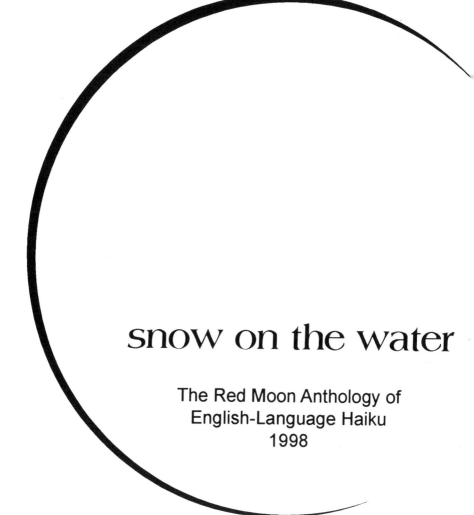

snow on the water

The Red Moon Anthology of
English-Language Haiku
1998

Jim Kacian ◊ Editor-in-Chief
Jan Bostok ◊ Tom Clausen ◊ Ellen Compton
Dee Evetts ◊ Maureen Gorman
Lee Gurga ◊ Yvonne Hardenbrook
H. F. Noyes ◊ Kohjin Sakamoto ◊ Jeff Witkin

Published by
Red Moon Press
P. O. Box 2461
Winchester VA
22604-1661 USA
redmoon@shentel.net

ISBN 0-9657818-8-7

All work published in
snow on the water:
The Red Moon Anthology of
English-Language Haiku 1998
by permission of the individual authors
or their accredited agents.

Special thanks to
Lee Gurga, Andrea Missias
and Neca Stoller for help
in the preparation of this volume.

Cover painting: *Black, White and Gray,* detail
Franz Kline, 1959: 30" x 22.25", oil on canvas;
The Metropolitan Museum of Art, New York.
Used by permission.

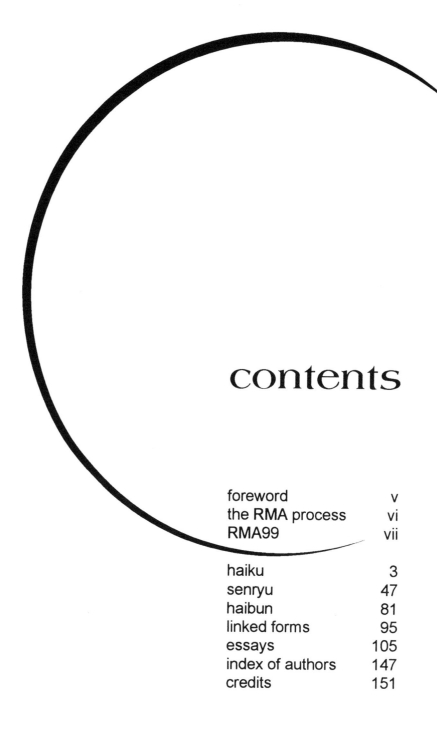

contents

foreword

1998 was a most interesting year in haiku publishing. Several books appeared which will be recognized, soon if not now, as seminal in their various genres, including Robert Bebek's *Oblici Praznine*, Lee Gurga's *Fresh Scent*, Jim Kacian's *Six Directions*, Sosuke Kanda's *An Owl Hoots*, Marlene Mountain and Francine Porad's *cur*rent*, Anthony J. Pupello's *The Saxman's Case*, Tom Tico's *SPRING MORNING SUN*, and Richard Wright's *Haiku: This Other World*, along with provocative anthologies from Canada (*Haiku sans Frontières*), England (*The Iron Book of Haiku*) and New Zealand (*The Second New Zealand Haiku Anthology*), and the first anthology of English-language haibun available to the general reader (*Journey to the Interior: North American Versions of Haibun*). These volumes appear prominently, as would be expected, in the pages which follow. Haiku journals weathered a year of typical flux, which reflects the difficulty that exists in making these fragile but important vehicles survive the economic and personal demands which they place upon their editors and publishers. The emergence of *Acorn* and *Snapshots* offset the disappearance of *Heron Quarterly*. Several others changed editors (*South by Southeast*, HPNC/*Woodnotes*), formats (*Haiku Novine*), or both (*Blithe Spirit*, *Frogpond*). Participation through these channels and on the Internet, which saw the emergence of several new haiku list groups and sites, was at an all-time high, and promises greater growth. The consequence of this interest for the editorial staff of *The Red Moon Anthology* was a record number of poems to be read, evaluated and ultimately selected. Over fourteen-hundred poems and related works were placed in nomination for this year's volume, and these ultimate 175 works reflect the best of the best of haiku and related work published in 1998. Enjoy!

—Jim Kacian, Editor-in-Chief

the RMA process

During the twelve months of 1998, over 1400 haiku and related works by nearly a thousand different authors have been nominated for inclusion in *snow on the water: The Red Moon Anthology 1998* by our staff of eleven editors from hundreds of sources from around the world. These sources are, in the main, the many haiku books and journals published in English around the world, and, increasingly, on the internet. (The list of sources at the end of this volume indicates all the books, magazines and other sources from which these 175 works were selected; there were also nominations from at least this many other sources that were not voted in to this edition.) Each editor is assigned a list of magazines, and the editor-in-chief is responsible for reading all sources (to ensure that all sources are considered by at least two readers). Editors are, however, free to nominate any work, from any source, they feel is worthy of inclusion. Editors may neither nominate nor vote for his or her own work. Contest winners, runners-up, and honorable mentions are nominated automatically.

When the nominating period concludes, all haiku and related forms which receive nomination are placed on a roster, and considered separately, and anonymously, in a vote of the ten editors (the editor-in-chief does not have a vote at this stage of the process). At least five votes are required for inclusion in this edition.

The editor-in-chief then compiles these works, seeks permissions to reprint, and assembles them into the final anthology.

RMA 1999

The Red Moon Anthology is an annual publication. Nominations are collected throughout the calendar year by each of the ten editors as well as the editor-in-chief for the subsequent volume. It is our stated goal to compile the best haiku and related work published or made available to a general readership in English each year.

Every attempt is made to be inclusive, and each magazine that regularly publishes haiku is assigned an editor. Nevertheless, thousands of haiku are published each year, and it is nearly an impossibility to ensure that every haiku receives its due consideration. This is especially true for the many books which are published, and in particular self-published, every year. In an effort to be exhaustive, we urge authors to send two review copies (one for the editor-in-chief, one for editorial assignment) to be considered for inclusion in *The Red Moon Anthology* to:

> Red Moon Press
> P.O. Box 2461
> Winchester VA
> 22604-1661 USA

Materials to be considered for the 1999 edition of the anthology must be received no later than November 1, 1999.

Only haiku which is being published for the first time will be considered for inclusion in the anthology. Reprints, reissues, retrospectives and commemoratives will not be eligible for appearance among the best poems of 1999.

snow on the water

haiku

 ai li ◊ Great Britain

accident site. . .
an umbrella
catching rain

 Suezan Aikins ◊ Canada

inchworm
just ahead of
evening shadows

5

 Nasira Alma ◆ United States

wind lifting
the quail tracks
with the snow

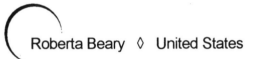 Roberta Beary ◊ United States

early spring walk
your hand
in my pocket

Edward Beatty ◊ United States

wind against
my pant leg—
cat gone for years

Mykel Board ◊ United States

the year's first
fortune cookie—
no fortune

Ernest J. Berry ◊ New Zealand

autumn
turning off the radio
to listen

late afternoon
the porch icicle
lit from within

Randy Brooks ◊ United States

funeral procession. . .
snowflakes blowing
into the headlights

Michael Cecilione ◊ United States

pausing between chapters
the sound of sleet
against the windows

Yu Chang ◊ United States

> starry night—
> biting into a melon
> full of seeds

Cyril Childs ◊ New Zealand

> firefly viewing—
> her feet. . .
>   feeling for the path

 Margaret Chula ◊ United States

late into the night
we talk of revelations—
moon through the pines

 Tom Clausen ◊ United States

Memorial Day—
overwintered in the sandbox
toy soldiers

David Cobb ◊ Great Britain

drip by drip
the moonlight lengthens
in the icicle

Ellen Compton ◊ United States

motor stilled...
the headland echoes
the loon

Helen E. Dalton ◊ United States

spring cleaning—
  behind the davenport
  the other Wise Man

Geoffrey Daniel ◊ Great Britain

a bitter rain—
two silences
beneath
the one umbrella

Helen K. Davie ◊ United States

on the path
only one of us
touched by a falling leaf

Cherie Hunter Day ◊ United States

alone. . .
in a porcelain bowl
winter spider

 Mike Dillon ◊ United States

     drought's end:
      the full moon ripples
     in the ditch

 Gene Doty ◊ United States

     winter night
     the mouse in the trap
     still warm

Bernard Lionel Einbond ♦ United States

> peeling an apple
> in an unbroken spiral—
> year's end

Jeanne Emrich ◊ United States

> dusk. . .
> the heron's slow step
> into shadow

Dee Evetts ◊ **United States**

clocks turned back
our Sunday walk
overtaken by dusk

Michael Fessler ◊ **Japan**

diving catch
some dandelion puffs
in center field

Garry Gay ◊ United States

Fading light—
the snake slips out
of its skin

Marshall Hryciuk ◊ Canada

hairpin turn
oncoming driver and i
watch the same eagle

Robert Gilliland ◊ United States

frosty moon—
silver of a possum's back
parting the ivy

abandoned chapel—
from its silent bell the buzz
of a nesting wasp

Lee Gurga ◊ United States

the smell of the iron
as I come down the stairs—
winter evening

winter prairie—
a diesel locomotive
throttles down in the night

a sunken barge
rusting in the shallows—
summer afternoon

Yvonne Hardenbrook ◊ United States

autumn leaves
each death-day of my son
                autumn leaves

poetry reading
  a baglady drops in
to warm herself

construction job
   workmen messing up
last night's snow

Christopher Herold ◊ United States

curling paint
shadows the lighthouse walls—
sound of the sea

driftwood
borne out again, again
and again

 Gary Hotham   ◊   United States

in what's left
of our footprints—
some of the wave

fog.
sitting here
without the mountains

eric l. houck, jr. ◊ United States

autumn wind—
the paper crane
sweeping from grandpa's hand

at her bedside—
watching the September sun
slide from her room

Jim Kacian ◊ United States

morning dew—
no hiding the way
we've come

cold snap—
a hairline crack
in the clay pot

ground fog
up to my ankles
in moonlight

25

Sosuke Kanda ◊ Japan

entering my
parents' room
winter sun

facing the wall
counting intravenous drips
end of the year

byron jackson ◊ Great Britain

everywhere
in the garden
three white butterflies

Glen Keener ◊ United States

an old schoolyard
some hollows in the ground
where the swings were

Michael Ketchek ◊ United States

> so much
> myself included
> hidden in the rain

Larry Kimmel ◊ United States

> after a hard look—
> the copperhead flowing
> into the stones

 Martin Lucas ◊   Great Britain

morning mist
a workman whistles
no particular tune

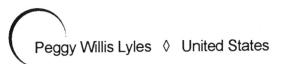 Peggy Willis Lyles ◊   United States

North Star obscured. . .
wild honeysuckle somewhere
in the dark

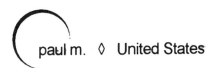

paul m.　◊　United States

falling leaves
the rusted wheelbarrow
heavy with stones

A. C. Missias　◊　United States

new grave—
the trampled grass
already recovering

 June Moreau ◊ United States

waking in the meadow
a lark's nest
an arm's length away

 Nikola Nilic ◊ Croatia

moonlight
river divides the forest
into two nights

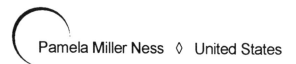

Pamela Miller Ness ◊ United States

after all these years
ankle deep
in the other ocean

Christmas Eve—
the row of cut trees
no one took home

H. F. Noyes ◊ Greece

waterfall—
the man with the booming voice
stops talking

Mark Alan Osterhaus ◊ United States

abandoned farm~
the scent of sweet grass
rising through the fallen porch

Tom Painting ◊ United States

ending
in wildflowers. . .
the logging road

D. J. Peel ◊ Great Britain

wintry evening
briefly the horse's breath
whiter than the moon

Anthony J. Pupello ◊ United States

this heat
the hooker's saunter
slows

Carol Purington ◊ United States

Deeper in woods
than the early light reaches
first crow call

Jeffrey Rabkin ◊ United States

> after coming in
> he opens the screen door
> to let a fly out

Emily Romano ◊ United States

> Sunday morning
> feeling the thunder
> through the bedsprings

Bruce Ross ◊ United States

coming to rest
the tossed pebble
takes a shadow

Timothy Russell ◊ United States

eggs sunny-side up. . .
shirtless men stripping
my neighbor's roof

Donna A. Ryan   ◊   United States

> gentle rain...
> the leaf mold's sweet scent
> rising with the mist

Doug Sherman   ◊   United States

> winter light
> the flowered wallpaper
> curls along a seam

 Ruby Spriggs ◊ Canada

my head in the clouds in the lake

 Elizabeth St Jacques ◊ Canada

first snow
the neglected yard
now perfect

 David Steele ◊ Great Britain

> shipping oars
> I hold my breath to hear
> snow on the water

 R. A. Stefanac ◊ United States

> frost predicted
>   the sizzle
> of fried green tomatoes

Wally Swist ◊ United States

dry season:
the mountain fire tower's radio
crackles with static

Brian Tasker ◊ Great Britain

in the park
a man and his boomerang
all over the place

Tom Tico ◊ United States

Christmas Eve . . .
at the lot, the trees
not chosen

Memorial Day:
wave after wave
hitting the beach

Cor van den Heuvel ◊ United States

after the grand slam
the umpire busy
with his whisk broom

Zinovy Vayman ◊ Russia

autumn evening
my hospital window
becomes a mirror

Teresa Volz ◊ United States

able to move
the whole herd
that one horsefly

Jeff Witkin ◊ United States

through tree shadows
the little fish loses
its own

Michael Dylan Welch ◊ United States

gridlock
    on the freeway—
the skywriting drifts

hospital room—
the crane's flight
through the wallpaper

sudden lightning—
  the street mime
    claps

Richard Wright ♦ United States

The crow flew so fast
That he left his lonely caw
Behind in the fields.

The Christmas season:
A whore is painting her lips
Larger than they are.

Just enough of rain
To bring the smell of silk
From umbrellas.

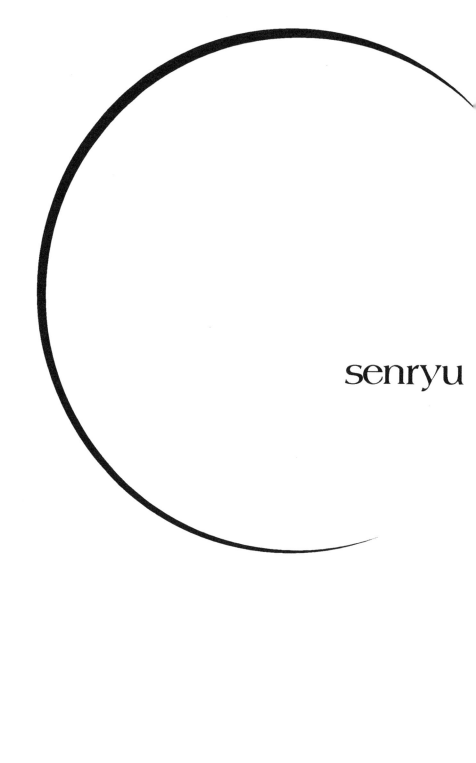

senryu

Ernest J. Berry ◊ New Zealand

impressive name
for a weed
i look again

Cathy Drinkwater Better ◊ United States

last day of the year
finally noticing the Monet
on the calendar

49

Miriam Borne ◊ United States

after the shooting
yellow tape around
the empty space

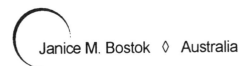

Janice M. Bostok ◊ Australia

test negative I decide to keep my promise anyway

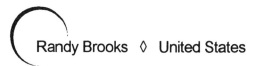

Randy Brooks ◊ United States

estate auction—
can't get my hand back out
of the cookie jar

behind her
up
the hayloft,
I watch
my step

James Chessing ◊ United States

> years in therapy
>   suddenly the old cactus
>   is blooming

Tom Clausen ◊ United States

> under the manhole
> the night gives
> a gurgle

Bruce Detrick ◊ United States

empty house
its great windows looking
out to sea

Frank Dullaghan ◊ Great Britain

on the teacher's apple
small teeth marks

Dee Evetts ◊ United States

> his dust mask
> a hole poked through it
> for the cigarette

Sandra Fuhringer ◊ Canada

> nightfall
> the zookeeper
> lets himself out

D. Claire Gallagher ◊ United States

blowing out
one birthday candle:
the whole family

David Gershator ◊ United States

at the flea market
looking through books
I gave away

Joyce Austin Gilbert ◊ United States

empty chair
his cat curls
into the imprint

Edward D. Glover ◊ Great Britain

On the great penis
of the fertility god
snow accumulates.

 Maureen Gorman ◊ United States

last hike
before the new job—
view from the overlook

 Doris Heitmeyer ◊ United States

cheap paperback
no typos
in the spicy parts

Yvonne Hardenbrook ◊   United States

classroom mineral chart
the fool's gold specimen
missing

what is whose. . .
at separation we both eye
the backscratcher

at the window. . .
as if that would bring him
                          sooner

Jim Kacian ◊ United States

rocking
back and forth
the conversation

Michael Ketchek ◊ United States

my father
losing his memory—asks me
not to forget him

Kenneth C. Leibman ◊   United States

even after Christmas
still wearing
the ratty slippers

Peggy Willis Lyles ◊   United States

I brush
my mother's hair
the sparks

 Makiko ◊ United States

home from abroad:
being met at the door
by my own smell

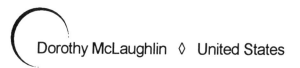 Dorothy McLaughlin ◊ United States

aunt's diamond ring
only she remembers
the dead soldier's name

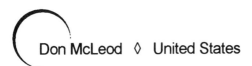

Don McLeod ◊ United States

the updraft
blowing his ashes
back to us

long wait over—
his thigh prints dissolving
on the lobby sofa

Paul David Mena ◊ United States

speaking with my ex-wife
I break open a peanut
and eat the shell

H. F. Noyes ◊ Greece

evening light
on the far white peaks—
newscast of war

Patricia Okolski ◊ United States

DOA
startling the nurses
his pager

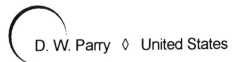

D. W. Parry ◊ United States

suddenly I realize
I've already crossed
the scenic bridge

 Carl Patrick ◊ United States

fireflies
my neighbor
has more

after ringing it up
the cashier sniffs
my sprig of mint

Dick Pettit ◊ Principality of Oran

the charity collector
eases open
a broken gate

Francine Porad ◊ United States

double plot
burying her husband
with his first wife

Anthony J. Pupello ◊ United States

simmering stew:
my wife's old boyfriend
comes to dinner

wedding vows:
the bride bats
her false eyelashes

Wall Street gym—
junior execs
run in place

William M. Ramsey ◊ United States

pulling gate nails
driven by
my young father

Alan Realey ◊ United States

still in my suit—
the smell
of the nursing home

Alexis Rotella ◊ United States

On our short walk—
her long list
of maladies.

Margaret Saunders ◊ Canada

the funeral director
sizing me up

Charles Scanzello   ◊   United States

hiking hand in hand—
both of us kicking
the same stone

Fred Schofield   ◊   Great Britain

children in the band
their silent faces
before the first note

Sharon Lee Shafii ◊ United States

convalescence ...
the goldfish swims round
and round the bowl

John Sheirer ◊ United States

talking in her sleep
my wife
calls someone stupid

Doug Sherman ◊ United States

long meeting—
one clock two minutes faster
than the other

Karen Sohne ◊ United States

scenic hillside
my daughter apologizes
for the absence of cows

John Stevenson ◊ United States

at the urinal
I remember my plants

the mirror
wiped clean
for a guest

between my rush to be ready
and her arrival—
a space

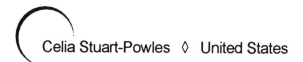

Celia Stuart-Powles ◊ United States

father's funeral
mother
suddenly small

George Swede ◊ Canada

Medieval town:
to the worn steps
I add my own

Diane Tomczak ◊ United States

family reunion
everywhere I look
my old nose

Charles P. Trumbull ◊ United States

grocery line—
the dancer's feet
in first position

Phyllis Walsh ◊ United States

talking to myself
another walker interrupts
talking to himself

David C. Ward ◊ United States

new employee
everyone smiling
once

Lorraine Ward ◊ United States

on the way
to the dentist
roadwork

Paul Watsky ◊ United States

science museum—
men's room towel dispenser
jammed

Nina Wicker ◊ United States

waitress serving crabs
one false nail
missing

Jeff Witkin ◊ United States

her Christmas bonus—
she uses it to buy me
out of the house

Nancy S. Young ◊ United States

walking together
step by step
and a half

Cindy Zackowitz ◊ United States

midnight—
I count the chimes
in spite of myself

haibun

Marjorie Buettner ◊ United States

In the Hospice

Louise was born eleven years before my mother-in-law and yet they are like old friends now sharing their last sleep in this room. Their body rhythms have been synchronized by the nurses: turning every two hours, a night bath, a morning massage. The faltering rise and fall of their jagged breath is a chorus I am trying to understand. Their cough, like the deep rumble of thunder, threatens to overwhelm as it travels closer and thicker everyday. Louise, who outlived everyone, was a teacher in the Dakotas; Rozella, a librarian, grew up there too. They both knew the dangers of an early spring, the bone-cold of winters not documented. But like this solitary bird in the dead-dark of this cold April morning, they both have, I am sure of it, a faith beyond instinct in possibilities unseen.

April Fool's day
my mother-in-law dying
with baby soft skin

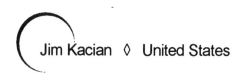

Jim Kacian ◊ United States

Custom

A mizzle does not deter the cyclists of Matsuyama. This is a city of bicycles, and one may encounter them at any hour on any street, and in any weather. Riders of all ages, in business suits and in tee-shirts, swarm the narrow streets, and the sidewalks of the major squares. Tonight they glide over the damp roads, leaving trails of treadmarks which shine in the light of the red paper lanterns which mark the neighborhood taverns.

Along Minami Edo, the major road into the railway square, the sidewalk is torn up for gasline repairs. Traffic is heavy, despite the late hour, and pedestrians and cyclists alike are forced onto a mud and gravel path alongside the road. At one particularly bumpy stretch, where pylons further constrict the flow of traffic, we are forced to one side of this makeshift path to permit passage of an elderly cyclist. The old man is moving too fast to stop in time, and we scuttle aside to prevent a collision.

The bicyclist, knowing the unfortunate pedestrians he has scattered likely will not have opportunity to witness his actions, does something extraordinary nevertheless. While maintaining his speed, he executes upon his bike a very deep bow, sustains it a moment (not easy to do because of the bumpiness of the terrain), then speeds off into the night. In the gloom of evening, the gesture is barely observable. But he performs it anyway. It is the thing to do.

We return to the hotel. It is late, and my travelling companion wants to write up some notes in his journal, read a bit, get to bed. We have another long day of travel ahead of us tomorrow. I'm a bit chilled from the April rain, and the call of the *onsen* proves too great for me. I head up to the seventh floor for a hot mineral bath. When I get there, I have the place to myself.

> all alone . . .
> my thorough washing
> before the bath

◊ ◊ ◊

The Curve of the Air

The meadowsweet is in bloom, and I cannot resist it: these dry hills and pastures are the places to walk by sun or moonlight. I roam the boundaries of the property, a long, slow circumambulation, and hear the meadowlarks from time to time lay down the spreading circles of their lilting call. Atop the highest of these low hills leading ultimately to the river, I hear the train whistle its approach, and each of the swales echoes with its music. I stand here long after the train has gone.

Along the southern property line is an old cemetery, perhaps once walled off from the woods, but now unbounded. The dates on the oldest stones are long effaced, but the family name remains prominent. The stone of the builder of Six Directions rests here, a little way off from the rest of the family. There is probably a tale here, but I do not know it.

> gnarled sylphium
> planted with the first bones
> blooms yellow

Later, as I walk the east pasture, I come upon a stray dog. Tagless and emaciated, fur badly matted, he is a shy and not quite wild beast, who apparently has been wandering for some weeks. He follows me home willingly, and, after some food, permits a little grooming—

> souvenirs
> of our far-flung travels—
> burdock bristles

Amenities finished, he makes himself at home on the thickest rug, in the warm shine of the midday sun. I suppose, now he has found me, he will keep me, and I him.

He is a happy creature, but silent in the main, who disappears according to a whim I cannot fathom and returns just as capriciously. The life he cultivates is a mystery to me. I do not understand why some animals seek man's companionship. Between man and most creatures there is at most an uneasy tolerance, an unhindered crossing of field or stream. Most or all of the mystique of wolf or bear, leopard or shark, has to do with its wildness, that is, its unwillingness to have commerce with man. But somewhere in the distant past a dog ventured in to a human's fire, a horse permitted a man to mount, and the ways of man and beast were changed forever. I have a certain disquietude about this, and prefer for the most part the wild ways of the other animals, their sense of being at home in their habitat, and their lack of dependency upon man's ministrations. But this dog is companionable, and we enjoy roaming these fields and orchards together.

Today we came upon an owl's nest in the beech woods at the eastern extremity of the property. The bird bolted suddenly, its wings churning through the air with a great roar, startling us both, making my heart pound and the dog yelp. This evening, overhearing its hunting cry, I recollect its fouled nest, and how its droppings glowed eerily in the dim light where it nested. And just now tonight a flock of blackbirds swarms to the branches of the low apple trees, filling in the twilit spaces until the crowns are opaque. Their natter and screech dominates the evening until darkness is fully established; then, only the occasional rustling of wings can be heard from them, as they settle into the wary sleep of the ever-hunted. This is a sort of wild domesticity, that seeks communion among its kind, and yet apart from the reach of others.

The dog ramps its ears in their direction, but they quickly go limp, and his eyelid droops. A moment later he is fast asleep.

cottonwood wind—
his measured breathing
in the lulls

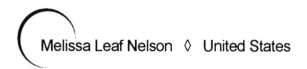

Melissa Leaf Nelson ◊ United States

Verdun

Clouds that had hung low and heavy for days, broke apart and gave way to clear skies as we drove into northern France. Dew on the Verdun battlefield glistened in the sun.

We stopped at a memorial to one of the nine villages that ceased to exist during the battle of Verdun in 1916. Homes, businesses, churches pounded into oblivion, leaving nothing to show that here families once worked, raised their children, lived, and fled. Not even the rubble escaped destruction.

The beauty of the day stood in contrast to the signs of the battle still evident after eighty years. What remains is the uneven terrain, where exploding shells ripped apart not just men, but the land itself. The land is still pockmarked. Pools of water collect in some of the larger shell holes. Signs today proclaim the stillness of the morning was broken only by the sounds of songbirds. The countryside was renewing itself as it does each spring. Everything green and growing pointed to new life, while the uneven land was still a quiet monument to death.

> birdsong—
> the shell-scarred earth
> beneath the grass

The air was calm. Nothing stirred. I too stood without moving. It was an effort to breathe. I wondered why some of the most peaceful places on earth are battlefields, when they were once places of so much horror. They call this hallowed ground. Nearly a million men were killed or wounded here. Numbers too large to fathom. Could it be their presence I am feeling on this morning?

> Verdun
> the stillness
> presses against me

And then a noise. Two military trucks in the parking lot faced the cemetery. Soldiers in fatigues and carrying machine guns walked slowly over this blood-steeped ground, faces full of concentration and contemplation.

> at the ossuary
> soldiers saluting the dead
> with their silence

Through the windows, a cairn of bones. Pieces of bodies were all that were left to remove from the battlefield and they were deposited here, gathered up by a solitary priest after the war. A skull with a jagged hole blasted into its side topped this mound of death.

These men were placed here together as there was no other way to do it. Too many bodies blown to bits. Impossible to piece together. Impossible to identify. Impossible to forget.

> heaps of bones—
> my tears so small
> beside them

High school students on a field trip disregarded the signs requesting silence and respect. They ignored the guard who motioned them to be quiet. They walked through the soldiers' memorial, grabbing at each others caps, laughing and jostling, unaware of their disrespect.

God forbid that they ever experience the horrors of war.

> World War I
> the war to end all wars
>   didn't

Patricia Neubauer ◊ United States

The Goldfish Vendor

The goldfish vendor
turned the narrow lane
followed by children
—*Shuran Takahashi*

The moment of pure delight is an ephemeral thing. One minute it is there, and the next—like the goldfish vendor—it has disappeared around the corner.

The daily duties and responsibilities of the adult world are governed by anxiety for the future. Scheduled work cannot be interrupted. The enjoyment of pleasure must be postponed until the appropriate time. When the goldfish vendor passes by, the adults look up briefly, shrug their shoulders, and turn back to the task at hand.

But children (and poets) know that delight does not present itself by appointment. Like a cat it comes when it will and must be taken up promptly lest it escape. The glittering gold having been glimpsed, the children are reluctant to let this enchantment slip away. They follow the vendor. They do not need a goldfish; indeed, they probably have not got the money to buy a goldfish; however, the joy of looking and longing is often greater than the joy of possession.

This small adventure of the children also offers the possibility of drama and suspense: who will buy the goldfish, and how much will they pay? Which fish will be chosen first? And so the children, indifferent to the past, unconcerned about the future, pursue their present happiness as long and as far as possible—until all the fish are sold, or until the vendor travels beyond the boundaries of their neighborhood.

Robin White ◊ United States

Drawing Down the Moon

In the center of a lunar garden, a bowl or bath of water is placed for the purpose of reflecting the moon, "Drawing Down the Moon," the Wiccans call it. The Druids used moon-ruled herbs such as cleavers, chickweed, wild poppy, and white roses to increase appreciation, awareness and sensitivity. Ponds half-hidden by woods are suddenly illuminated by the Hunter's Moon, as are the gentle ripples of puddle-water, the mosquitoes and fireflies dipping in and out. And in both the Waxing and Waning Moons, blue herons have been witnessed performing movements as graceful and deliberate as Tai Chi.

> noting in my journal
> that mountains too
> live on the moon

Rich Youmans ◊ United States

Sunday Visits

I never knew my grandfather when his words were clear as spring water and spiked with a brogue strong as Irish whiskey: the man with the lilting tenor, who sang rebel ballads as he carried the day's mail; who argued daily with the corner grocer over the price of pears, then overpaid with a flip "Keep the change"; who at weddings sang out toasts with the abandon of a child, and over pints at O'Fenn's wove boyhood tales of Ireland—of nights spent in the sweet smell of peat fires, when his own grandfather would recount the heroics of Wolfe Tone, Emmet, Pearse, and Collins.

I knew him only after his second stroke, his lilt gone, his left leg strapped to a brace. By that time he had moved in with my aunt and spent most of his hours in the living room, on a sofa the color of weak tea, staring into the fireplace. We visited every Sunday evening. Always, my parents followed my aunt into the kitchen to help with dinner, leaving me on the sofa with my grandfather. He would speak to me, sounding as if he were underwater— the gargled syllables of a drowning man, incomprehensible. Occasionally an understood word or phrase bubbled through—"How's school?"—from which I wove whole conversations about my teacher's unkempt beard and my attempts at long division and Friday's hot lunch and anything else I could think of. But usually I couldn't understand a thing, and simply nodded and agreed: the last refuge of the baffled.

I think he saw through me, though, for sometimes he would abruptly laugh and slap my knee; I, of course, would laugh with him. And other times he would look away into the fireplace, at pale brick blackened by soot, and say nothing at all. . .

> twilight. . .
> shadows seep into
> grandfather's quiet

◊ ◊ ◊

Hale-Bopp

Ann and I stand on our front lawn, our faces tilted toward stars and deep space. We have been out here for fifteen minutes, staring at nothing but the constellations, and I am already growing tired. But not Ann. All week she has been looking forward to this night, when Hale-Bopp could be seen for the first time in 4,000 years. "The last time it came, the Great Pyramids had barely been built," she'd say. "The next time, none of us will be here." I'd smile, happy in her happness, but unable to fully share her awe.

Now she searches for the comet, its flaming tail. A light wind passes through nearby birches. Ann keeps scanning the sky. "I think that's a planet," she says, pointing toward a steady white dot just above our neighbor's chimney. I nod. Behind us our house stands solidly: an earth-bound presence, comforting. The soft sound of a jazz sax filters from the stereo, and I think of the music drifting toward the heavens. I gaze up, imagining myself as one of those notes

> our small house
> under galaxies—
> all the windows lit

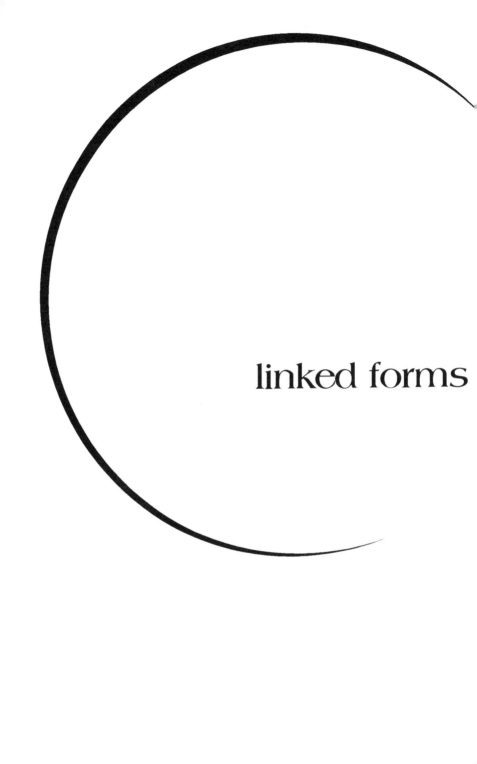

linked forms

Cathy Drinkwater Better ◊ United States

Only the Groundhog

visiting day
the old nun licks gnarled fingers
to find the sign-out sheet

with sideway glances
they eye me as I wait:
my daughter's schoolmates

through the double doors
her old swagger
only on Saturdays now

white dogwood blossoms
seem to float—a sister
waves and smiles

breaking old habits—
the whiteclad nuns
walk the grounds in pairs

the tour:
white wrought-iron benches
"where the penguins sit"

fresh tunnels—
only the groundhog
comes and goes

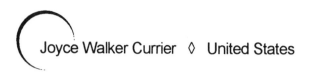

Joyce Walker Currier ◊ United States

the gift of a book

the gift of a book
inside the jacket cover
his winter haiku

sharing lunch
we speak of the stages
of his cancer

restaurant window
table now empty
where we sat

seeking my old friend
between the lines
of his haibun

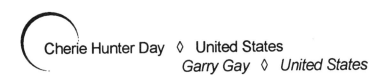

Cherie Hunter Day ◊ United States
Garry Gay ◊ United States

Snapshot

cropped photograph—
leaving my shadow
on the darkroom floor

from the bottom of the tray
your smile slowly develops

pullling me closer
in front of the camera. . .
first date

pinned
on the bulletin board
your snapshot

a roll of negatives. . .
the brightness of your dark eyes

self-timer
I join you
in the photograph

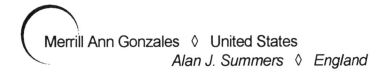

Merrill Ann Gonzales ◊ United States
Alan J. Summers ◊ England

Into Sunlight

into tropical air
rainbow lorikeets—
a mango restaurant closed

temperate cardinal
chipping his latin beat

at 45 degrees
the driving rain
filling a beggar's bowl

these evening showers
in a field of bare trees

the clouds turn green
when snared on eucalyptus. . .
the sacred ibis

raising its wide wings
exposing a sunrise

pointing eastwards
twitching in a dream
the dog's paws

chasing ruddy deer
through rainbows

morning's warm moist air
curls around my legs
unseen caress

river reeds rustling
someone comes through the shadow

a dozen crows fly
above the lone cyclist

sparrow on a branch
listening to wind blow
where does it come from?

filling a white sail
bending a tree

holding ancient forms
roots seeking clear waters
under the earth

above the street & stark trees
a gap in clouds: the moon

gentle light bathes
the opened chrysalis
strange new light

in the distance
sacred ibis rise from grass

sudden thunder
black butterfly flitting
from flower to flower

broken cobweb
a moth flies away

dream changes
on my pillow
black and blue dust

mudprints
across a white bedsheet

the shroud
of a child
before cremation

dirt and dew
glistening pumpkins

stones for the cairn
above   the cardinal
claims his old branch

turning, a smile seen
night draws in

so far away
in the deepest darkness
a beacon on the hill

candle out
the sizzle of saliva on fingers

pointing the thread
only the hole can receive
for the needle

unravelled into the wind
kite of many ghosts

first flight
after the broken wing healed

Catherine Mair ◊ New Zealand
Patricia Prime ◊ Australia

Day Out

leaving Katikati opossum's fur colour of autumn leaves
by roadside hedgehog dwarfed by mountains
Whangamata wharf beneath his straw hat their father baits the lines
footprints in the sand all different sizes
towards the entrance lift and dip of paddles
boys cast rods in unison
behind his pumping legs child on the aqua cycle
over horizon kayaks disappear one by one
sniffs my writing pad spots on the spaniel's nose
in the forest car laden with surfboards
Selwyn throws pebbles into grass the cat pounces
the way home knowing all the icecream stops

Jeff Witkin ◊ United States
John Stevenson ◊ United States

The Bow Unravels

New Year's day
a man in a top hat
unplugs the tree

the ball drops
in Times Square

opening gifts
the bow unravels
and her gown slips away

nearly everyone
crossed off
the list

snowball mows down
a row of icicles

children
coiled with anticipation
a wishbone snaps

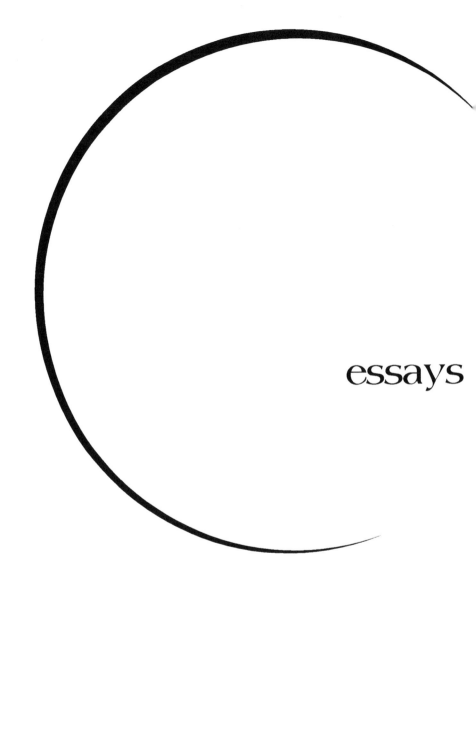

essays

Rich Krivcher ◊ United States

Writing from the Monkey Face

> year after year
> on the monkey's face
> a monkey face

How can I paraphrase Bashō's penetrating obviousness? On first reading, when I came to the end of the second line, I expected that Bashō would then show me something incongruent "on the monkey's face"; but the incongruence was in the way I previously saw or imagined a monkey face—and everything else for that matter. On top of an 'original face' I had placed a coarse image, what I thought was a monkey face. I hadn't really seen.

Reading this poem led me to ponder the notion of mask. I thought of Greek drama: the comic mask of Thalia, the tragic mask of Melpomene. I thought about the severe expressions of the Japanese Noh masks and the wrathful masks of Tibetan Buddhist deities. I thought of Hwui Shan's account of men in a far distant land who had human bodies and animal faces.[1] I thought of the *masque*—the aristocratic revel of pantomime, dance, and song in Shakespeare's England.

I thought of Al Jolson singing in blackface; I thought of Eddie Murphy singing in whiteface.

I thought of Bette Davis in the movie *All About Eve*, in which she plays a famous stage actress, Margo Channing. At the beginning of the film, Margo is seen resting in the dressing room after a masterful performance, her face greased, denuded of cosmetics, as she leisurely smokes a cigarette and exchanges tart remarks with her entourage—but who else could it be but Bette Davis!

I thought about a friend, slightly older and deeply philosophical, whom I had not seen for five years. Within the last couple of years his ideal marriage had disintegrated into an agonizing divorce. When I saw him anew his face had aged more than those five years would have warranted. Aside from the greyer hair and the more deeply etched lines on his forehead, recessed black semicircles under his eyes seemed to expand the sockets into large dark teardrops. Within those teardrops his eyes shone with the softness and vulnerability of one who has known a most bitter truth.

I thought of a girlfriend who routinely—and may I say, happily—fashioned a flawless, elaborate face every morning before going to work only to wipe it clean again every night before bed. I remember the cucumber freshness after the scrubbing.

I thought about my rolfing treatments and the particular session when the rolfer attempted to free the fascia, the connective tissue, that had bound itself to the muscles of my face. I recalled the localized pain along the underside of the cheekbones extending down to the hinges of the jaw; then the shudder at recognizing that the cheerful, smiling face with which I faced the world was nothing but a mask—glued and set.

That night after reading Bashō and allowing these sensations to drift in and out, as I lay in bed waiting for sleep a string of words, a ready-made haiku, was forged in my mind. The words like a final punctuation seemed to complete my thoughts:

> night after night
> the mask removed
> reveals a mask

For a number of weeks this summary expression was self-satisfying. Eventually, though, I had to acknowledge that my poem is founded upon the hopelessness of ever discovering a true, uncompromised identity. In contrast, Bashō's poem is about the clarity of seeing and knowing, immediately, without question. What is there is there. The mask is removed, if indeed there ever was a mask, because preconception no longer clouds perception.

What is it, though, about Bashō's poem that works so well, that pins this reader right between the eyes? The subject, a monkey face, is both well known and distinctive; Bashō transposes the distinctive onto the well-known. If I could simply remain true to Bashō's formula, I reasoned, and insert a visual subject with similar qualities, then perhaps I could create a poem of similar effect. By attempting to reconstruct the artistic process, I further reasoned, I might garner a deeper appreciation of Bashō's art and learn to convey a truer vision. I thought long and hard, for the better part of a day, of a fitting image. At last, these lines emerged:

> scene after scene
> on Groucho's face
> a Groucho face

Admittedly, Bashō's monkey face is more naturally archetypal and the effect more penetrating, but for all these years haven't we taken for granted Groucho's face, a veritable symbol of comedy? Haven't we all donned those half-masks—the cheap plastic glasses with the hollow plastic nose, busy eyebrows, and mustache—and pretended to be Groucho? Hasn't Groucho's face become for us a caricature of Groucho's face.

Despite this minor success at mimicking, or should I say *aping* Bashō's poem, I couldn't stop there. I wanted to expand the scope of Bashō's formula to other sense impressions and to return to a more serious vein. I reminisced how as a young boy in Tennessee I often was overcome on summer nights by the cacophony of crickets and cicadas and other unidentifiable buzzings, especially near my favorite lake. I used to walk there by myself, after supper, and just listen. If I listened long enough and intently enough my perceptions would sharpen and within the silence of all that unearthly chattering I would hear more than I ever could have imagined. Inspired by these ponderings, with haiku I conclude, at least for now, an extemporaneous study of Bashō's "monkey poem":

> on this summer night
> in the cricket's call
> a cricket calls

---

1. Hwui Shan was a Chinese Buddhist monk who reported to the Chinese court in the year 499 A.D. on his travels in Fusang, a country far to the east of China. In her book *Pale Ink* (Chicago: Swallow Press, 1972), Henriette Mertz presents a fascinating, though often fanciful, argument that Fusang was none other than the North American continent and that Hwui Shan, after arriving from China by boat, traveled throughout the southwestern United States and Mexico. Mertz postulates that Hwui Shan's description of men with animal heads refers to ritual costumes which native Americans wore to celebrate the totems of the tribe. Mertz also writes of an earlier exploration in North America by the Chinese in the twenty-third century B.C. See also Charles Godfrey Leland, *Fusang, or The Discovery of America by Chinese Buddhist Priests in the Fifth Century* (New York: J. W. Bouton, 1875).

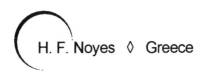

H. F. Noyes ◊ Greece

Simplicity, Spirit & Speculations

The purple poppy
Turns its head
With each breath of wind
Ion Codrescu

waving back
at the poppy field
the retarded child
vincent tripi

poppy—
both of us
simply alive
Issa (arr. by tony suraci)

These poppy haiku wonderfully exemplify that simplicity which is at the heart of the haiku spirit. Note how at the same time they illustrate, on a deeper level, seven of Robert Spiess's finest "speculations."

1) In genuine haiku we live as if for the first time, fresh and innocent, knowing reality through deep feeling.

2) Haiku employ a now-moment's material phenomena as a point of departure for reverberations reaching into interior modes of existence.

3) Haiku are written best and appreciated best through the intelligence of the heart.

4) A haiku is not meant to convince the intellect but to engender what may be termed an "affirmation" in the very ground of one's being.

5) The greatest pleasure given by an authentic haiku's object-perception as such is always less than the least of the joys offered by its spirit.

6) Haiku is the poetry of the healing of culture by nature. (Gloss on words of William Irwin Thompson.)

7) The entities of haiku are natural sacraments.

Great Haiku with *Sabi*

To Alan Watts, *sabi* was close to that state of detachment in which we see things as happening by themselves in a kind of miraculous spontaneity.[1] It's a state of acceptance, in which aloneness evolves into a sense of all-oneness. Our wholeness is restored when we "let go" and, as Chuang-tzu expressed it, "let everything be allowed to do as it naturally does." Zen teaches "Do not on any account interfere with the natural course of life." When her son died, Tombô (Lorraine Ellis Harr) found something reassuring and even in a measure healing in the sheer fact that the world went right on turning. And she wrote this, in *Dragonfly*—a genuine haiku moment, not a metaphor:

> A hot summer wind—
> shadows of the windmill blades
> flow over the grass[2]

How well this Virgil Hutton haiku illustrates William Higginson's description of *sabi* as "beauty with a sense of loneliness in time."[3] An extraordinary sense of stillness is achieved in this eternal moment:

> Dusk over the lake;
> a turtle's head emerges
> then silently sinks[4]

Charles B. Dickson wrote a number of death poems before his passing. I find this one, that seems to shut out all life and light, a farewell most redolent of *sabi*. (Yet rain ends, a key opens a car, and his spirit lives on.)

> rain-swept parking lot
> headlights of a locked car
> grow dim[5]

I highly prize this haiku with a haunting *sabi-aware* element. Because Adele Kenny lets nature speak for itself, the connection is made in an unforgettable way between death and the ongoing stream of life. A classic.

midsummer morning—
the dead tree's shadow
stretches upstream[6]

There are haiku of *sabi* that can engulf us in a limitless sense of desolation and aloneness, haiku that we feel from the bottom of the heart. Charles D. Nethaway Jr., shares with us the most vulnerable and defenseless haiku moment I can remember:

how many times
did I tell him to be quiet—
child in coffin[7]

Watts spoke of *sabi* poetry as having a quality of "quiet, thrilling loneliness," and of deep moments "swallowing all sound." James Minor's haiku classic captures the solitude of that "locked out" feeling of late night hours.

such is night
no door
no key[8]

1. *The Way of Zen*, p. 186.   2. July 1973.
3. *The Haiku Handbook*.   4. *Haiku World*, William J. Higginson, editor, p. 137.
5. *Modern Haiku*, Summer 1991.   6. *Haiku World*, p. 105.
7. *Wind Chimes* 12, "For Daniel Nethaway, 1975-1983."   8. *Wind Chimes* 22.

Tom Tico ◊ United States

Personification

One doesn't find many instances of personification in English-language haiku, but already there have been a number of gems. In some poems the personification is subtle and hardly noticed; in others it is full-blown and cannot be missed. The following span the spectrum of those two extremes.

1

> In a muddy rut
> dark water harbors visions
> of the Milky Way
>
> *O Southard*

Hinduism tells me that I am not the individual with whom I so readily identify. I am not this thin and aging persona known to myself and others as Tom Tico. I am Brahman; I am the all-pervading spirit of the universe. I am Satchidananda; I am existence, knowledge, and bliss absolute. And a day will come—or a night—when I will awaken to my true self, when I will transcend the muddy rut of my life and fully experience my cosmic identity.

2

> The rusty wind-chimes
> wait quietly for the music
> of a summer breeze . . .
>
> *Tom Tico*

The rusty wind-chimes have weathered so much, and still they hang at the end of the slender chain: receptive, compliant, faithful. It seems as if the wind will never come; even a breeze would allow the chimes to fulfill their purpose. But, alas, there is only the still and oppressive heat of summer. So, the wind-chimes wait, quietly, stoically, bearing their lot . . .

3

spring night
this newborn moon
swaddled in haze
            George Ralph

The association that immediately comes to mind is that of the Christchild being wrapped in swaddling clothes and laid in a manger. Therefore the poem implies that the Christ consciousness is not just limited to Jesus but is a force latent in all of nature. The fact that the moon is new, and also the year, presages a great spiritual development that has only just begun.

4

No warmth, no color—
the moon favors my garden
with nothing but light.
            Marjory Bates Pratt

Drawn to her garden by the beauty of the full moon, the poet is engulfed by its light. Not only is there no warmth and no color, there is also no sound and no movement, everything is perfectly still, including the poet, who stands transfixed in an ecstasy of light. Never before has she felt such wisdom and serenity, such an elevation of spirit. Surely the goddess has bestowed her grace, and the poet's heart is full of gratitude.

5

darkening path
the white morning glories
lead the way

Wilma M. Erwin

Death is near, and the poet moves towards it with faith and fearlessness. She thinks of how William Blake died singing; and how the soul of St. Francis was accompanied by the skylarks. She hopes that she too will have a beautiful death. She is convinced it will not be an end of consciousness but   an expansion—a further flowering of her being.

6

Slowly the sun leads
the old man and crooked cane
down the mountain road.

Joanne Borgesen

That "God is Light" is an ancient idea common to many religions, therefore it isn't surprising that the sun is often perceived as a symbol for the Most High. Seen in this light the poem indicates that the old man with the crooked cane is following a path that the Great Spirit wishes him to tread. And despite his infirmity, the old man valiantly and steadfastly adheres to the way.

---

1. *Marsh-grasses* (American Haiku Press, Platteville WI 1967).
2. *Haiku West* 1:2, 1968.
3. *frogpond* XIX:1, 1996.
4. *American Haiku* III:1, 1965.
5. *frogpond* XV:2, 1992
6. *American Haiku* VI:1, 1968.

J. P. Trammell ◊ United States

Haiku:
Toward an Organic Definition
for the West

I.

Haiku Sensibility: the Spirit of Community

What is a haiku? If we in the West accept at face value the essays and published haiku we read, we might conclude that a Western haiku can be "anything we please." Operating within the framework of Western poetics, the well-intentioned Westerner severs haiku from its Japanese roots and merges the genre with conventional Western lyric poetry. As a result, in the West, haiku's distinction blurs and haiku is no longer discrete among the poetic genres.

Of course, not every Westerner merges haiku and lyric poetry, but—as Raymond Stovich pointed out nearly a decade ago in "Six Approaches to Haiku—a Developmental Schema"—our haiku community tends to fall into "antithetical camps."[1] One camp desires to maintain Japanese haiku tradition (while debating what this means); another advocates expansion of haiku tradition to encompass Western poetics. Unfortunately, when Western poetic theory, process, and convention define haiku, its identifiable elements disappear, making haiku impossible to distinguish from Western lyric poetry in both technique and expression. However, to understand the distinction between haiku poetry and Western lyric poetry, we may look into the heart and temperament of the cultures out of which these genres have grown. To this end, it is helpful to distinguish between the intuitive spirit of community (which engenders haiku) and the discursive spirit of individualism (which engenders lyricism). If we can establish the difference between haiku and lyric poetry, we may infer the sensibility and spirit of both haiku poetry and the haiku poet's perception, defining those characteristics which must manifest if haiku is to survive its transplant from East to West.

What is the essence of Japanese perception? In relation to the Japanese sensibility, Thomas Kasulis, an Asian studies scholar, proposed this Buddha narrative: When Buddha peels back the leaves of the banana tree, he finds "no center—only emptiness." Buddha, who sees the banana tree as a sign of life's ephemeral, transient nature, accepts the comfort of this emptiness. The banana tree, in the Japanese tradition of identifying it with Buddha nature, symbolizes the way of perception.[2] In contrast, the essence of Western perception might be symbolized in Henrik Ibsen's dramatic scene in Peer Gynt[3]. When Peer Gynt peels away the scales of an onion "to the innermost center," he is appalled to find "nothing" but emptiness.[4] Already in despair over his dualism, Peer Gynt sees the onion as nature's ironic confirmation of the Self's isolation and meaninglessness, thus pitting himself against the cosmos. The onion, in the Western tradition of identifying with the rebel, symbolizes the idea of perception. A basic agreement between the Japanese and Western cultures might be that the centers of both plants symbolize emptiness, but the respective implications of this conclusion are radically different: what brings spiritual comfort to the Japanese only intensifies the Westerner's malaise. But how does this transfer to the aesthetic of haiku?

The comfort of eternal emptiness, the void at the center of the banana leaf or the onion—this is the essence of haiku. All parts of the way of haiku, experience, intuition, image, and brevity offered through language merge, to share with another the poet's momentary comfort in the universe—the eternal emptiness transformed into shared communion.

The Japanese sensibility, with its aesthetic and empathetic character, is synonymous with the intuitive temperament, which has been finely honed over centuries of putting the good of the community before the individual's welfare. The intuitive mind accesses truth through non-rational means; intuitive intelligence trusts and acts upon knowledge which has no empirical basis because intuition is informed by direct perception rather than sequential deduction. There is no identified process for intuition—it 'happens' based on mechanisms which are, as yet, little understood.* Empathy, an important facet of intuition, describes the physical rapport and response which accompanies an intuitive perception.

On the other hand, the Western sensibility, with its strong empirical emphasis, is synonymous with the discursive spirit, bred through centuries of regard for the rights of the individual. The discursive intelligence, motivated by cause and effect, premise and conclusion, is bound by the process of "logical connection" between ideas. Effects must proceed from causes by logically demonstrable proofs. When logic no longer generates connections between ideas, they are deemed unrelated. To the discursive mind, truth cannot be separated from logic. And, while the individual may sense "personal" truth, the transferability of personal, mystical experience is an impossibility to the discursive intelligence. This has profound implications for the modern Western poet and for lyric poetry. Primary among these is the poet's isolation, not only from other individuals, but from nature (the cosmos) itself.

Since culture defines aesthetics, the pervasive insistence on logical connection in Western thought also characterizes Western poetics. Structured by rational criteria (chiefly, the development of the poem's imagery by chronology and/or

*However, the reader will be interested in these observations made by Editor Spiess when reviewing this essay: "...true, that there is no identified process for the occurrence of an intuition, but there seems to be some sort of predisposition or 'ground' for an intuition to occur in any particular person. For example, I could never have had the intuition of relativity that Einstein had because I do not have sufficient grounding in physics; or the 'ability' to have the intuition of what the structure of benzene is, as Kukulé did, who, after years of pondering over the problem, had a dream (a form of intuition!) of an ouroboros (a snake swallowing its tail), which gave him the full intuition or realization that benzene consists of a ring of 6 hydrogen- carbon molecules. So it seems that some kind of 'requirement' is needed for haiku intuition to occur--it probably is only the practice of being closely perceptive and sensitive to nuances in entities."

association, and the abstraction of the concrete image into a figurative one), lyric poetry becomes a vehicle for the expression of the poet's personal, emotional labyrinth: lyrics of separation, alienation, frustration, and pain issue forth as do the songs of caged birds. In contrast, haiku crystallizes a moment of time and experience characterized by intuitive connection with the life-force, which does not begin and end with the individual, but, in Japanese tradition, is part of a transitory continuum of a larger universal fabric. Indeed, R.H. Blyth sees the divide between East and West as epitomized in the Buddhist and Christian religions, "the Buddha in eternal peace and the Christ in eternal agony...."[5]

Thus, even an abbreviated analysis of the respective cultures giving rise to haiku and lyric poetry reveals a sharp delineation between these forms: haiku springs from intuition and perception, while lyric poetry is born of ego and song.

In 1800, William Wordsworth proclaimed the fusion of the poetic and individualistic spirits. In his "Preface to Lyrical Ballads" he articulates the seminal Romantic credo, which, to this day, is basic to the composition of Western lyric poetry. Defying classical tradition, Wordsworth proclaims that good poetry

> ...takes its origin from emotion recollected in tranquility: the emotion is contemplated till, by a species of reaction, the tranquility gradually disappears, and an emotion, kindred to that which was before the subject of contemplation, is gradually produced, and does itself actually exist in the mind. In this mood successful composition generally begins, and in a mood similar to this it is carried on....[6]

Further, the concerns of the individual, Wordsworth exclaims, are the true stuff of life and poetry; in fact, man gives meaning to the cosmos, and not the cosmos to man:

> ...I should mention one other circumstance which distinguishes...[good poetry]; it is this, that the feeling therein

> developed gives importance to the action and situation, and not the action and situation to the feeling.[7]

Such assertions found fertile ground in the late eighteenth century "revolutionary fervor" which swept through Europe and the United States (epitomized by the French and American Revolutions), and fused poetic theory and expression with the pursuit of Self-centered consciousness and its most precious commodity, individual liberty.

Because Western man operates from a perspective which suppresses the intuitive faculty, he identifies haiku—poems based on intuitive perception—as just another mode of lyric poetry (lyric poetry is defined as a genre characterized by relatively brief, subjective verse displaying deep feeling or intense emotion). One respected professor and scholar, James William Johnson, commenting on haiku, designates it as "the most concise kind of lyric poetry ever devised."[8] So, despite the vast differences in the cultures out of which haiku and lyric poetry have evolved, is it possible, nevertheless, that haiku is merely another lyric form, subject to the lyric conventions of subjectivity, abstraction, association, and reflection? Many in the West believe so. One English language haiku poet (Raymond Stovich), recounting the manner in which he composed the following poem,

> after the argument
> hearing the drizzle
> all night long[9]

echoes the process described by Wordsworth (above). Stovich explains that his poem had its genesis in a mood inducing the "need...to write something"; next, the poet conjures his past through an extended, associational linking of images (he hears a dripping faucet, associates it with winter rains in Northern California, which bring to mind Midwestern drizzles, etc.).

Following the methodology described by Wordsworth, the poet, on a quest for personal truth ("about my life") dredges powerful emotion from the past, rekindles, focuses, and shapes it into what would seem to be a lyric poem. Nevertheless, applying the traditional, associational method of lyric composition to haiku, may a haiku still somehow result? Individuals deemed worthy of judging haiku thought so, as the poem (the author tells us) "won two awards."[10] Yet, the poet evokes imagery from mood (as opposed to moving from the objective image to mood); the poem's "truth" is arrived at through a series of associational exercises, rather than by direct perception (in other words, there is no "haiku moment"); and its images are connected logically. In essence, "after the argument, I heard the drizzle all night long" does not conjoin dissimilar images, but rationally and chronologically connected ones. So, while I like the poem and respond to it, I respond to it as lyric verse and not as a haiku.

When Samuel Coleridge, a seminal voice of the emerging Romantic sensibility, notes that "Poetry without egotism" is "comparatively uninteresting,"[11] he summarizes a dominant element of the Western poetic perspective: since poetry "without egotism" (as haiku aspires to be because ego inhibits the intuitive faculty) minimizes the personality of the writer, it is an unsatisfying vehicle for the expression of the individualistic spirit. For, while Keats and others of the High Romantics espouse empathy's virtues, the balance in their poetry tilts sharply toward the subjective; with lyrical outpouring, these poets sing of the Self's subjective truth. But, as every Japanese knows automatically, subjectivity blunts the intuitive faculty, and self-absorption precludes empathy—one cannot empathize with the pine tree who does not sense its being and pause to share its spirit.

II.

Haiku Poetry: An Organic Form

The distinctiveness of the cultures which engender the haiku and lyric forms defines their differences. So apprised, let us now undertake, point-by-point, a discussion of the following haiku definition for the West: a haiku is a brief poem, ordinarily spoken in a single breath; characterized by objective-world experience, it records an instant of heightened perception realized through intuition and empathy.* Since haiku is an intuition-based poetic form, the manner in which the intuitive faculty manifests dictates the definition's elements.

Intuition and Empathy

The haiku poet's "instant of heightened perception" is "realized through intuition and empathy." But why? As we have noted, the cornerstone of the Japanese ethos is "community." Community implies cohesiveness; gravitation toward a central norm is far more important in the communally-based society than any premise set forth by the individual. Typical Japanese accept the idea of a natural order, external to themselves, shared by members of the community. This valuing of the community above oneself directs the intuitive and empathic faculties outward, so that they are attuned to reading the moods and needs of others, or to understanding the essence of things. In the West, by contrast, intuition is suspect because it has not been modeled and verified empirically. So, for the typical Westerner, the intuitive faculty, walled in by rationalism, simply lies dormant. But haiku—encapsulated moments of quint-essential intuitive experience—are poetic manifestations of the Japanese community ethos, and the maintenance of community vitality (including poetic aesthetics) depends on the utilization of empathy and intuition. The former is essential to understanding how others feel, while the latter, conjoined with empathy, guides understanding and response. Empathy and intuition denote the existence of a shared universe, where, as Bashō suggests, we may learn of the pine tree from the pine. Great haiku spring from this mode of perception. To quote but one:

---

*Of course, this discussion presupposes that the poet's images are drawn from his\her personal objective world experience. Harold Henderson notes with astonishment that Shiki (1867-1902) had to remind the haiku "Masters" of his day to "gather new material directly." In Henderson's words, that this "advice...would have been thought necessary...certainly shows the depths to which haiku had fallen" in Shiki's time.[12]

The summer grasses—
Of brave soldiers' dreams
The aftermath

Bashô[13]

Fused by Bashō's empathy, the fragile grasses and man's fate are one.

Objective-world Experience

The intuitive element of haiku is a product of the reaction between the poet's intuitive intelligence and some objective-world phenomena; however, in view of Western lyric theory, a rationale is required for this assertion. We begin with the questions, to what extent should haiku be composed of objective-world images? To what extent may haiku images be drawn from the artist's subjective world? And, we must add, given current Western aesthetic theories that disavow distinction between subject and object, does it even matter? The rationale for subject-object dissolution is summarized in the following thesis:

> ...the subject matter of a haiku may...legitimately be an experience of the imagination (philosophically, this statement rests upon the understanding that differences between subject and object, perception and imagination, inner and outer, etc. are projections of our own concept-making minds).[14]

However "logical" this may seem to the Western intelligence, from the perspective of the Japanese intuitive intelligence, intuition itself establishes the realness of objects of perception. In Japanese culture, individuals recognize that there is a clear distinction between their subjective world and the world outside themselves, of which they are a part and not the source. Thus, the "imagination" does not dissolve external reality for the Japanese; rather, it mediates aesthetic balance between the inner and outer worlds. In haiku composition, "objectivity" and "imagination" are not mutually exclusive concepts. The imagination functions as a factor of intuition. Unless the poet engages intuitive differentiation between subject and object, the imagination cannot mediate aesthetic balance, and its marvelous, autonomous power of discrimination and selectivity is stifled. As many in the West have noted (including T.S. Eliot),[15] experience, to be transferable in poetic terms, must be characterized by some element of the external world which becomes a touchstone, some thing mutually knowable by poet and audience which will identify the experience in time and space. (If this is true for all poetry, then it is true the more so for haiku, with its extreme brevity.) Of these touchstones or common denominators of experience, those concrete objects and phenomena outside ourselves which may be interpreted through the senses are the sole possibility.* More critically, it is our interaction with elements of the objective world which triggers the type of intuitive experience known as the "haiku moment"—those inexplicable instants of aesthetic, spiritual, or psychological insight which are conveyed to the reader through the juxtaposition of logically unrelated sensory images. From such secure ground, the reader's intuitive faculty may leap into the collective pool and make the right connections to re-establish the tenor of the original haiku moment—this is the haiku "leap of faith" required of both poet and audience.

Haiku Brevity

Haiku brevity is understood in view of the nature of the intuitive faculty, which manifests in flashes of insight, unanticipated understanding, triggered by unexpected events acting powerfully upon the perception of the individual—this is the so-called "haiku moment," the "instant of heightened perception." To the extent that the haiku moment is brief, the form that conveys it must be brief, or the impact of the experience is lost and its shared resonance broken.

---

*The role of "nature" and the "season word" in haiku composition requires more exhaustive treatment than is permitted in this essay. Here, suffice it to say that the Japanese embrace an expanded concept of nature that includes not only the "natural" universe, but, also, human thought and activity in their myriad manifestations. Still, because the Japanese revere nature through the empathic Shinto spirit and this reverence infuses their aesthetic ethos, we must acknowledge a special place for nature imagery in haiku. For, of all that which is external to us, it is the natural world alone which, in its perpetual Being, reflects the Eternal Present and suggests the embodiment of Eternal Presence.

To conclude, "organic" denotes an interrelation of "parts" fused into a single entity, whose connection is analogous to the organic unity of living systems. In any organic definition of haiku, all components are interrelated and interdependent, to the extent that if a single element of the definition were eliminated, its cohesion would collapse. The suggested definition meets these criteria.

> *A haiku is a brief poem, ordinarily spoken in a single breath; characterized by objective-world experience, it records an instant of heightened perception realized through intuition and empathy.*

As addressed above, without intuition and empathy, there is no haiku. If the intuitive faculty is not engaged, the interplay between self and Other (interaction with the objective world) will produce no new aesthetic, spiritual, or psychological awareness—there will be no instant of heightened perception, no haiku moment. And, since brevity of haiku form derives from the instantaneous nature of the haiku experience, it follows that the intrinsic value of haiku brevity is attached to its capacity as a vehicle for intuitive experience—simply, a form is needed that may reproduce the lightning impact of the haiku intuitive flash.

AFTERWORD

What makes the haiku poet?

Time and again, as I am struck favorably by a particular English language haiku, I observe that it offers what one might call (in Western terms) "nonrational synthesis." In spite of the polarizations which dictate most Westerners' response to experience, these authors are able to convey a sense of life's multifaceted connectedness, perceived in patterns as variable as life itself.

Haiku such as,

daffodils the lightness of being uninlove[17]

a quiet day
an old man on his tractor
passes at dusk[16]

Marlene Mountain

sagging footbridge—
on both sides of the brook
white laurel blossoms[18]

twilight storm
another stone topples
from the pasture wall[19]

Charles Dickson

Becoming dusk,—
the catfish on the stringer
swims up and down[20]

a rainbow's remnants
at the far end of the marsh—
where the moon will rise[21]

Robert Spiess

The silence
of paper lanterns:
morning rain[22]

Discussing divorce
he strokes
the lace tablecloth[23]

Alexis Rotella

Shadows in the grass
our feet grow cool
as we talk of lost friends[24]

Cheeses, pâté
my mouth suddenly dry
when she looks at him[25]

Rod Willmot

while disparate in their moods and concerns, yet, without abstraction or artifice, convey intuitive synthesis arrived at in an instant of heightened perception. The reader senses a secure, creative, intuitive presence operating behind each of these poems. Through the skillful enjambment of disparate images, each poet—buttressed by a refined aesthetic—conveys feeling and insight by fusing intuition and artful expression—without resorting to discursive technique. This is demonstrated Oneness of essence and form: it marks the master poet's work.

REFERENCES

1. Raymond J. Stovich, "Six Approaches to Haiku—a Developmental Schema,"*Modern Haiku*, Vol. XX, No. 1 (Winter-Spring) 1989, pp. 10-15.

2. Observations made by Dr. Thomas Kasulis at the East-West Center (Honolulu) on June 16, 1995, at a NEH seminar on Japanese culture. Dr. Kasulis is Professor of Comparative Studies and Chairperson of the East Asian Languages and Literature Department at Ohio State University.

3. Henrik Ibsen, *Peer Gynt, Collected Works* (Volume X), trans. W.J. Black, Blue Ribbon Books, New York NY (1928).

4. Ibsen, act V, scene v, p. 582.

5. R.H. Blyth, *Zen and Zen Classics*, The Hokuseido Press, Tokyo (1960), p. 123.

6. William Wordsworth, "Preface to Lyrical Ballads," *The Poetical Works of Wordsworth* (Cambridge Edition), Houghton Miffin Company (1982), p. 797.

7. Wordsworth p. 791.

8. James William Johnson, "Lyric," *Princeton Encyclopedia of Poetry and Poetics* (Enlarged Edition) ed. Alex Preminger, Princeton University Press, Princeton NJ (1990), p. 430.

9. Stovich, p. 14.

10. Stovich, p. 14.

11. S.T. Coleridge as quoted by David Perkins, ed. *English Romantic Writers*, Harcourt Brace, Fort Worth TX (1995), p. 15.

12. Harold Henderson, *An Introduction to Haiku*, Doubleday Anchor Books, Garden City NY (1958), pp. 152-53.

13. Makoto Ueda, *Bashô and His Interpreters: Selected Hokku with Commentary*, Stanford University Press, Stanford CA (1991), p. 242.

14. Stovich, p. 14.

15. See T.S. Eliot's famous essay , "Hamlet and His Problems," in which he coins the phrase, "objective correlative"—in *Selected Essays*, Harcourt, Brace & World, New York (1950), pp. 121-126.

16. Marlene Mountain, "a quiet day," *The Haiku Anthology* ed. Cor Van Den Heuvel, Simon & Schuster, New York N.Y. (1986), p. 152.

17. Mountain, "daffodils," *Modern Haiku*, XXIV, No. 3 (Fall 1993), p. 22.

18. Charles Dickson, "Sagging footbridge," *Haiku Moment* ed. Bruce Ross, Charles E. Tuttle Company, Inc., Boston (1993), p. 38.

19. Dickson, "twilight storm," p. 39.

20. Robert Spiess, "Becoming dusk," *The Shape of Water*, Modern Haiku Press, Madison WI (1982), p. 21.

21. Spiess, "a rainbow's remnants" (unpublished), used by permission of the author.

22. Alexis Rotella, "The silence," *Haiku Moment*, p. 204.

23. Rotella, "Discussing divorce," *The Haiku Anthology*, p. 201.

24. Rod Willmot, "Shadows in the grass," *The Haiku Anthology*, p. 293.

25. Willmot, p. 292.

A special thanks and sweeping credit are due Robert Spiess. Although I do not cite his *New and Selected Speculations on Haiku* (1988) and *A Year's Speculations on Haiku* (1995), I have drawn deeply on them in ways both evident and intangible.

Anita Virgil ◊ United States

Issa: The Uses of Adversity

> My Spring?
> A single bamboo—
> A willow twig.[1]

Kobayashi Issa (1763-1827) carved out a singular piece of turf apart from the other major haiku poets. His work is an amalgam of earliest haiku, Bashō's haiku, senryu and tanka uniquely tempered by his Pure Land Buddhist beliefs and often put together in what today would be called a "confessional" mode. Superficially, his poems (as read in translations, albeit) look easy to understand: many are sentimental and laced with humor. This has made one of Japan's most revered haiku poets attractive to writers who wish to experiment with haiku. But what we accept as Issa's "haiku" hinges upon his unusual life story without which many of these well-known prototypes appear woefully shallow and misleading. However, once a correlation is drawn between this poet's life and the various guises in which he portrays it, certain poems which appear trivial transmute into poignant utterances.

> So hospitably
> waving at the entrance gate—
> the willow tree.[2]

This poem offers little to the reader but a pretty picture hardly worth recording. What insight has it? What significance? Really none. But once we learn Issa's family home had a willow tree at its entrance, and due to the machinations of his stepmother Issa was barred from it for some forty years, this poem changes. Its effect is completely altered to depict bitter irony and sadness. Now its significance is obvious. And it is heavy with emotion.

Because Issa is referred to as one of the Four Pillars of Haiku and the poet closest to the heart of the Japanese people, reading a poem of this type (and many such by Issa are translated into English) leads one to assume that as it stands it is an exemplary haiku. This immediately creates a problem if you happen to feel as I do that a haiku ought not to depend solely for its impact upon the crutch of outside information. For this reason, I have been disappointed by much of Issa's work and considered many of his "haiku" to be anomalies. The problem stems from the fact that when these poems are judged on their own merits minus biographical explanations, they come up short. Of course it is true that with Bashō and Buson, added dimension may devolve out of an awareness of some details of their lives, but most all of their haiku stand up without this extra information. Further, it is doubtful that some of the "haiku" of Issa would have the very special cast they have without the groundwork laid by the emergence of the senryu in the 18th century. Many of his poems are full of senryu's biting sarcasm, of the rising political and social consciousness. They are replete with a human emphasis and use the spoken everyday language of the senryu. There are also love poems—those written at the time of his first marriage late in life venture into a realm eschewed by haiku poets. The tanka and certain stanzas in renga were considered the appropriate place to elaborate on this subject. Or, depending on the cast of the poem, in the senryu.

In fairness to a poet who has given us some astonishingly powerful and beautiful poems that conform to the constraints inherent in haiku, poems which arouse deep emotion without recourse to Issa's psyche for their impact, we are obliged to learn more about Issa's life to understand those other poems of his which, for years, I chose to dismiss in favor of such as these:

> The spring day closes,
> Lingering
>   Where there is water.[3]

A straw-mat;
The Milky Way aslant
In the saucepan.[4]

The foal
Sticks out his nose
Over the irises.[5]

The turnip-puller
Points the way
With a turnip.[6]

The *yamabuki**
Hidden by the grasses—
And then again they sway.[7]

A day of haze;
The great room
Is deserted and still.[8]

Wild persimmons,
The mother eating
The bitter parts.[9]

This world of ours!
Even the grasses over there
Give us our gruel.[10]

Twilight spreads
From the woman waiting on the shore
Over the evening tide.[11]

The next poem is about a beggar:

In his box
Four or five coppers, and now
The evening drizzle![12]

---

* *Keria japonica*, a plant with yellow miniature mum-like flowers

These poems indicate the range of Issa's vision of the world and his feelings about it with, for him, uncommon elegant austerity and delicate humor. They unite the ordinary with the beautiful, the mundane and the heavens above which is perfectly consistent with Issa's attitude towards life. The grand, the minute, all co-exist. The dignity and identity of each object is allowed to come through to the reader. The turnip-puller brings out Issa's veneration for the nourishers of the world. The simple incredible beauty which man always seeks to hold onto is exposed only briefly to him—somewhere between the whim of a breeze, the length of a grass clump. In this poem about the *yamabuki* there is more of an elegy to the lost things of this world than in Issa's maudlin attempts to demonstrate it elsewhere. Such is the compass of the best haiku.

Grandeur and loneliness go hand in hand in the great-room poem with an overriding mysteriousness. As for his wild persimmon, at last Issa can express motherhood, the best of it, by focusing on a single act that embodies the whole range of caring he so yearned for. Acceptance and gratitude for our portion—whatever it is—is the foundation of the next poem, "This world of ours!"

For me, the woman-at-twilight poem is one of the greatest love poems, positively primordial in tone. Its sensuous quality is so diffuse it is like music—the stirring moving gloom and scope defy description. One is engulfed in it—yet it is no more than a woman at twilight, waiting. The last poem about the beggar has all of Issa's life story implicit in it, but happily, we do not depend on that information to derive full value from this haiku. All these exemplary haiku illustrate the region in which this tiny poem surpasses other poetry: its ability to suggest the vast in one thing. And all the information needed to understand these poems is contained within them.

The early life of an individual sets up the pattern of his existence. Chance, too, plays a role in how things turn out in the long run. It would seem the cards were stacked against Issa almost from the beginning. But the true measure of any man is determined by how he handles what is dealt him.

Kobayashi Yataro (Issa's childhood name) was born on May 5, 1763. His father, Yagobei, was a farmer who owned extensive lands. His mother, Kuni, also came from a farm family of substance. His birthplace to the north and west of Edo (Tokyo) was the beautiful village of Kashiwabara in the mountainous country of northern Shinano (now Nagano). Three mountains rose to the north and west of the village and Lake Nojiri spread out in the east. It was a snowy region of Japan where farming had to be carried on between April and October—before the land was buried in whiteness. Even the flowers adapted to the harsh region:

> The nine-belled flower
> Here bears only four or five bell-blossoms
> And that's all![13]

The village was located on an important route from the north which made it a vital center for travellers going between the great feudatories. The village was declared part of the Shogun's territory and was administered by Edo. Despite its seeming isolation, Kashiwabara was host to all sorts of people whom the child, Issa, observed. Among them were the mighty *daimyō* and their retinues on their way back and forth between the capital city and their own lands.* These great processions inspired a group of poems in which Issa gave voice to social criticism. One approach was the sarcasm of senryu:

> What's that to me,
> His million bales at harvest?
> Dew on a grass stalk![14]

> Following in his train
> Come the mists that swirl and trail—
> Kaga-no-Kami![15]

---
* This constant travel forced upon the *daimyō* by the Tokugawa regime was for the purpose of controlling them. With their families held hostage in Edo, the *daimyōs'* coffers were depleted by the expenses incurred on these journeys. That way, they could not amass sufficient funds to raise an army against the Tokugawa regime.

Both these poems refer to Maeda, Lord of Kaga, before whom all bystanders were supposed to bow in deference. The grandeur and pomposity of it all is apparent—but Issa's attitude is less than respectful. Subservience was not a high priority with Issa any more than were the conventions of a society he found wanting. Seeing the common people forced to pay homage to these dignitaries did not sit well with Issa, the son of hard-working farmers. Here is an indirect approach typical of Issa's social criticism poems:

Little sparrow! Take care!
Get out of the way!—Mr. Horse
is coming there![16]

By the time the young Issa was three years old, his mother died. The impact of her death apparently never was far from the mind of the boy or the man. Issa himself wrote in later years that he became a peculiar child, lonely and unable to adapt to the other small children his age who had their mothers and fathers still. Even though Issa's grandmother was good to him after his mother's death, his adult poetry still rings with this desolate feeling of deprivation, of a loss of nurturing. In poem after poem Issa gnaws this bone: maternal admonishments, childish entreaties fill them. Were it not for the other dimensions of his work, one would be hard-pressed to find the excess bearable.

Come! With each other
let's play—little sparrow
without any mother![17]

When the boy was eight years old, his father married a woman by the name of Satsu, a tough, hard-working woman determined to make a success of the large farm. Issa had made some headway in his schoolwork by this time and found comfort in the attention of his teacher, Nakamura, a man who was to remain a lifelong friend. The stepmother soon became resentful of Issa's scholarly pursuits. She expected him to be a farmhand and before long saw to it that her husband, Yagobei, took the boy out of school. Issa was worked all day on the farm and at night had to make straw sandals. He was forbidden to have light by which to read or write during the long winter nights. His hatred of his stepmother is reflected in such non-haiku as

> Somebody you do resemble—
> The face, at least, is much the same
> Death adder![18]

The chastisement he received from Satsu for any infractions relating to wasting his time with studies appears in this poem:

> O world of men!
> Even for writing on a leaf—
> Again a scolding![19]

The teacher he befriended held classes at the inn frequented by travellers so that whenever the boy could sneak away to visit Nakamura, he also widened his view of life beyond the farm.

In 1772 Satsu gave birth to a son, Senroku. This turned out to be a further burden to the already miserable Issa. Now, in addition to the hostilities he called forth from his stepmother, he was held responsible for much of the care of his infant half-brother. Nothing Issa could do would please Satsu. He was beaten daily, he later wrote, and "never slept without shedding tears."[20]

At last his father came to realize the situation between his wife and his first-born son, Issa, was impossible. With what today seems an act of weakness, Yagobei sent his son alone to Edo at the age of fourteen. He did, however, accompany the boy to the next town on the route and left him with the following admonition: "Eat nothing harmful, don't let people think ill of you, and let me soon see your bonny face again."[21]

And so the young Issa made his way into the capital city of Japan. He had a letter of introduction to one of his mother's relatives in Edo but he never followed up on it. It may be that he worked as a stable boy in one of the mansions of the *daimyō* stationed in Edo. This poem vividly shows the influence of senryu as do many of his socially conscious poems:

> They sleep
> on new mosquito nets—
> Horses at Edo.[22]

They fared far better than the homeless stable boy.

The young man must have matured very rapidly left to fend for himself, and illusions about mankind must have deserted him quickly. Apparently, he made friends in priestly orders and got to know enough of life in the temples around Edo to view them critically.

> The temple so clever
> At raking in the money—
> It has the peonies![23]

The society into which Issa was born was degenerating—on the downside of the cycle which followed the brilliant Genroku age. Town life depicted in his poems shows that he was alert to the variety of experience a teeming metropolis offers.

> Don't mention people—
> Even the very scarecrows,
> Crooked every one![24]

> The Servants Day—
> The house-dog also sees them off
> Into the mists.[25]

Servants Day (or *Yabu-iri* as it is called) occurs once a year at which time servants are expected to return to their farm homes for a visit. We know the house-dog, at least, returns to a home of comfort and luxury when the goodbyes have been said—but the servants? Many became drifters after a few years of city life or were simply too old to be re-employed.

Floating weeds
As blows the winds of the floating world—
Drifting and drifting.[26]

It is believed Issa entered the Katushika school at the age of nineteen. The school supposedly was founded by a close friend of Bashō and it is here, almost ten years later, Issa succeeded his teacher, Nirokuan Chikua, upon his death. At this time, the following poem is attributed to Issa.

All I saw
Through the perspective glass*
—Threepenny worth of mist. [27]

Again we see the harvest reaped by Issa from the senryu. Again we read between the lines and find the disappointed child—expecting something marvelous, Issa's lot is mist. The poem, objectively written, contains undertones of Issa's bitterness disguised by wry humor. The poet has shown us both our naive hopefulness and what, in fact, we receive.

But the conventionalism of the school did not allow for this sort of poetry. Issa's lectures were also unorthodox and complaints were made against him. Within a year, he resigned his position. It was at this time Issa became considerably concerned about his father and returned to his home in Kashiwabara. Yagobei was well and happy to see his long-departed son. Plans for a long journey—a pilgrimage in keeping with the tradition of literary figures—were shared with Yagobei who approved. It is in 1792 that the name "Issa" was adopted for the first time—more specifically, Haikaiji Nyudo Issa-bo (Brother Issa, Lay Priest of the Temple of Poetry). This was commemorated in the following announcement—I would not call it a poem.

Here's the Spring
And with it transmogrified
Yataro becomes Issabo.[28]

---

* The telescope was quite the novelty in 18th century Japan. In some of the Ukiyo-e prints of the same period it can be seen in use.

136

The journey which lasted until 1798 took Issa through the western provinces and Japan's southern islands of Shikoku and Kyushu. Issa visited temples, befriended priests and poets, merchants, much as Bashō did before him. A record of this is in the journals by Issa which were filled with tanka, haiku, prose passages, some Chinese poems from which he drew for later collections. Upon his return to the capital, Issa befriended an influential man named Natsume Seibi who was a wealthy rice merchant. They shared an interest in haiku. Seibi, supposedly possessed of an excellent critical sense, remained Issa's close friend and literary confidant for the rest of his life. Issa sent drafts of his work to Seibi for criticism over the years.

By 1802, when Issa was 39 years of age, he ventured back to visit his father at Kashiwabara. While Issa was there, Yagobei contracted typhoid fever. Issa nursed the old man for a month and though no stimulants were to be given him, somehow he drank wine and death soon followed. During his last days, Issa's father attempted to mend the split between Issa and his half-brother. Senroku, who expected that Issa as the eldest son would receive the major inheritance, was still dissatisfied. After all, it was he and his mother who stayed on and worked the farm all the years Issa was exiled. Yagobei "gave Issa a written document and made him promise to settle down and marry at Kashiwabara. This will the stepmother and Senroku afterwards refused to recognize and so bilked Issa of his inheritance for nearly thirteen years."[29]

> Once again in vain
> his mouth he opens— the bird's
> stepchild.[30]

The bitterness toward this unending miserable familial relationship ate into Issa. Though at one point he decided to legally resolve the problem, Issa unwisely gave the document his father wrote to one of the village elders along with a written promise elicited from Senroku to divide the property. Not surprisingly, all the documentation disappeared.

During this time Issa was still in Edo living a meagre and untidy bachelor's existence in his hut.

> If the times were good,
>   I'd say, "One more of you, sit down,
>   flies around my food."[31]

> Spiders in the corner—
> Don't you be anxious,
> I won't break your webs. [32]

He made no concessions to the niceties or expectations of society. This rebelliousness (probably born of injustices over the years) helped alleviate some of Issa's old anger and anguish as did his acerbic wit. He seemed to flaunt his pariah's existence for it freed him from social restraints. If Issa was by all indications an outsider, he made the most of it. In an odd way it enabled him to act upon the dictates of his own heart which resulted in that endearing perversity of Issa's which thumbs its nose at the formalities and trivial concerns of men.

> The bright full moon;
> My ramshackle hut
> Is as you see it. [33]

> The snail
> Goes to bed and gets up
> Just as he is. [34]

It is not at all strange to find him playing out an ancient hurt by siding with the underdogs and bucking authority. Even the mighty Maeda, Lord of Kaga (the same one of his early childhood), bent to Issa, the poet, in these later years. His Highness had commanded his presence but Issa refused to respond until such time as it was conceded that it was an invitation, not a command! When Issa showed up, it was in his scruffy clothes.

How agreeable it is,
My cotton gown—
Now it is soaked with sweat! [35]

A bush warbler comes:
all muddy are the feet he wipes
upon the blooming plums. [36]

I would like to digress here in order to suggest an interesting interpretation for the above poem hinging on a device writers so often utilize: the protective mask of indirect personification. The bush warbler is a bird noted for his beautiful utterances, just as the poet is noted for his. The plum blossom was the emblem of the Maeda family—Maeda, Lord of Kaga. By implied personification Issa can alter entirely the light and charming tone of the primary interpretation of this haiku to satisfy his persistent psychological obsession. Here, however, subdued personification has not undercut the haiku's quality. This interpretation is just something I read into it for the tactic of the veiled jab is not unknown to writers throughout the centuries: Jonathan Swift's *Gullivers Travels*, Franz Kafka's *The Trial*, Harriet Beecher Stowe's *Uncle Tom's Cabin*, each disguised political, social criticism. Issa, like a court jester, could cleverly present the truth and get away with it.

At the end of the visit, Issa was given several rolls of cloth as a gift. When he arrived back at his hut, he discarded them. On another occasion he was given a writing box of sandalwood by Lord of Kaga. One can see that despite Issa's eccentricities, he was admired and respected even by the mighty.

But in his village in the snow country, he still amounted to nothing. Finally, in 1812, Issa wound up his affairs in Edo and moved back to Kashiwabara. In a desperate attempt to rectify the legal situation, he petitioned the Shogun since his family property was on Tokugawa land. By this action he stood to lose everything, but with the intervention of an abbot, a compromise was reached. All was split literally in half—including the very house which was partitioned by a wall down the middle! Poems such as the following are the result of these times:

Old village, my home,
Everything I touch about you
Turns to a thorn! [37]

Is this, then,
My last resting place—
Five feet of snow! [38]*

In 1814 Issa at last married a twenty-eight year old neighboring farm girl by the name of Kiku.** Thus Issa fulfilled the other half of his father's will. It is from this courtship that Issa's love poems stem. One does not ever get the impression that the marriage was other than one of deep affection and passion.

Feet for a pillow
And our arms intertwined—
The tenderness of deer! [39]

For all the pain and loneliness endured, Issa at last shared with Kiku what had so very long been denied him: warmth and love, tenderness and good humor.

There's our Kiku—
A lot she cares, how she looks,
how she goes! [40]

'Our home—'
Just saying that alone—
What coolness! [41]

A careful look at these three poems which, *because Issa wrote them*, are considered 'haiku', will show that in actual fact they come closest to senryu in subject matter and handling. Along with their human emphasis, occasionally senryu will contain a season word, but even so, the emphasis on nature in them is missing. So it is with these. In the first, Issa uses the

---

* This poem appears on Issa's gravestone.
** *Kiku* means chrysanthemum in Japanese.

word "deer"—a season word implying autumn. But what he is actually doing is implying simile (as tanka do) to make the point that he and his wife's gently entwined limbs are manifestly *like* the tenderness of deer. In the second poem we have the season word "kiku" (chrysanthemum) by which the Japanese imply autumn. But Kiku is Issa's wife's name, and I am certain that were she named for a flower designating a different season, Issa would have done the same thing because season has little bearing on this poem either. It is an affectionate portrait of his wife and speaks to her devil-may-care attitude about her appearance. That is its entire point. The last poem utilizes the word "coolness" which is a season word for summer. But what the poem is about is the psychological state of relief arrived at as represented in the opening phrase "Our home—" which Issa is saying is as wonderful, as salutary as coolness on a hot day. Knowing what we now know of the poet who has been homeless most of his life, we must realize where the weight of the poem lies. It is redolent with Issa's past.

Issa's marriage occurred at a time in his life when he had finally earned a great reputation in the capital of Japan. His poems were highly influential. "It was at last recognized that his strength and simplicity had brought something back to poetry lacking almost since Bashō's death, and if it was his quaint insect poems that first caught popular fancy, the grave elegiac music of others stayed longer in the listening mind."[42]

What of these "quaint insect poems"? The following three examples are among the most well-known.

> Oh, don't mistreat
>   the fly! He wrings his hands!
>   He wrings his feet! [43]

> For you fleas too
> The night must be long,
>   It must be lonely. [44]

> Cry not, insects,
> For that is a way
> We all must go. [45]

Some other insect poems:

> Be a good boy
> And look after the house well,
>   Cricket! [46]

> Now I am going out;
> Be good and play together,
>   Crickets. [47]

> Grasshopper,—
> Do not trample to pieces
>   The pearls of bright dew. [48]

Though each of these six poems is a *cri de coeur*, none is handled with the self-effacement, the selflessness sought by the haiku poet. In all these Issa foists upon his insects human emotions and behavior thereby corrupting the Buddhist tenet which gives value to both the animate and inanimate. Not all creatures are human, though. A grooming display of a fly involves no beseeching as Issa would have us imagine. Nor can fleas be assumed to experience loneliness or insects sadness as depicted in poems #2 and #3. These are mere poetic fancies, intellectualizations, conceits in which Issa adopts the persona of an admonishing and loving mother which diminishes both the poet and the insects. The basic weakness of these poems is their blatant personification, a device which was not the province of haiku from Bashō on. They are throwbacks to the conceits of Sōkan (1465-1553) and Teitoku (1571-1653), to seminal haiku like this one:

> Don't be swallowed up, frogs
> Into the stomach
>   Of the snake in the eaves![49]
>   Ichiwa (pre-Bashō)

Compare to Issa's famous entreaty

> Lean frog,
>   don't give up the fight!
>   Issa is here. [50]

It was the pre-Bashō poets whose frogs, like cartoon characters, "rubbed their hands together" and "sang *sedōkas*" to whom Issa is reverting and to some poor quality senryu and these bellicose mosquitoes:

> The flies withdraw from their position,
> And the mosquitoes raise their war-cry.[51]

Issa clearly uses these same devices to make us sympathize with the weak of the world as represented by the "insignificant" creatures he so often writes about. But I think those handled in this manner are his least valuable works. I recognize wearily that cute has always been more popular than acute. For this reason they appear more often than his stronger work and therefore have come to represent Issa to many people. But he is too good a poet to be remembered for pandering to sentimentality.

Issa took liberties with the haiku to suit his own needs which, to a certain degree, is what all "originals" do. But in ignoring the constraints of haiku utilized by Bashō and other masters, Issa's poems caused me great confusion at the outset. For the advancement of understanding haiku, I feel it is important that writers especially pay attention to the standards consistently manifested in the work of the great poets when we seek direction and inspiration. It is also beneficial to have an historical perspective so we can recognize the underpinnings of their art.

Here is a very different insect poem by Issa:

> The first firefly!
> It was off, away,—
> The wind left in my hand.[52]

In this one Issa has objectively captured the essence of the moment: one of sudden beauty—and after, when all that's left is the remembering. That is what a firefly is. That is what a genuine haiku is. This haiku has "the grave elegiac music which stays forever in the listening mind."

Issa, as a now-famous poet, was often away from home, but his letters to Kiku expressed his continuing love. Before long, their first child was born—a son who lived but one month. His second child, a little girl named Sato, was born the day he returned home from a journey. Some of his child poems are about this daughter who only lived two and a half years. She succumbed to smallpox. The following poem was written after Sato's death and is one of Issa's most famous works:

> The world of dew—
> A world of dew it is indeed,
> And yet. . . [53]

In this poem allusion is made to the Buddhist doctrine of the transitoriness of life ("A world of dew") against which Issa of the Pure Land Buddhist sect rails in the grief-ridden, so very human poem. No religious precept can quite come to grips with the bone-chilling finality of the death of those we hold most dear. All man's anguished protest lodges in those two words "and yet. . ."

Again we have a vivid demonstration in this poem of the dependence in Issa's work upon knowledge of his life story—he even put a pre-script to it which read "Losing a beloved child." Without this, the poem is little more than a platitude.

A year after the death of Sato, another baby was born who lived only briefly. Issa's health was failing at this time and from the year 1820 on he suffered attacks of paralysis. When their fourth child was born, Kiku became ill and finally died two year later in 1823.

> The moon tonight!
> If only she were here
> My old grumbler! [54]

As though all this pain were not enough, the fourth child also died "by reason of the carelessness of the woman employed to nurse him. She turned out to be the daughter of the village bully who had tormented Issa in childhood."[55] Two other marriages ensued. One lasted only a few weeks and then the woman, a lady of *samurai* family, left Issa. In 1825 he married a woman named Yao. In the summer of 1827 a fire burned down Issa's family homestead. Offered housing by friends, Issa and Yao declined and stayed in a windowless narrow storehouse which was to be Issa's last home.

> A world of grief and pain,
> Even when cherry blossoms
> Have bloomed.[56]

In November, though Issa had been ill, he recovered sufficiently to visit pupils and friends again. On the 19th, after a walk in the snow, Issa suffered his last attack of paralysis and died. Under his pillow this verse was found:

> A blessing indeed—
> This snow on the bed-quilt,
> This, too, is from the Pure Land.[57]

Issa wrote 20,000 poems—far more than Bashō and Buson put together. (Buson wrote about 3,000.) Issa's sheer volume speaks more of catharsis than of craftsmanship. Of the variety of Issa's poems available to Western readers, it appears to me he wrote three very different kinds of poetry. Unfortunately, it is all presented under the umbrella of haiku. One kind manifests the aesthetic constraint which does belong to the special province of haiku. Another whose primary focus is clearly on human nature (whether treated humorously or not, containing so-called season words or not) is senryu. And the third which, no doubt, is responsible for Issa's broad appeal as a vulnerable human being to whom all can relate, is a pure *cri de coeur* that cannot seriously be considered as haiku when characterized by unrestrained emotionalism, intellectualization, and a failure to stand alone without explanations. These run counter to Bashō's advice: "But always leave your old Self behind, otherwise it will get between you and the object." Too often, Issa cannot. Poems of this type may have had therapeutic value for the poet, but they do not compare favorably with his few great haiku nor with his excellent senryu. When he had control over his various obsessions, his artistic genius shaped enough work into a parcel to add to world poetry.

1. Lewis Mackenzie, *The Autumn Wind* (London, John Murray Ltd., 1957), p. 53.
2. Harold G. Henderson, *An Introduction to Haiku* (Garden City, NY, Doubleday & Co., Inc. 1958), p. 140.
3. R. H. Blyth, *Haiku*, Vol. II, Spring (Japan, Hokuseido, 1950), p. 38.
4. —, *A History of Haiku*, Volume I (Japan, Hokuseido, 1963), p. 388.
5. —, *Haiku*, Volume III, Summer-Autumn (Japan, Hokuseido, 1952), p. 188.
6. —, *Haiku*, Volume IV, Autumn-Winter (Japan, Hokuseido, 1952), p. 348.
7. Mackenzie, *op. cit.*, p. 52.
8. Blyth, Spring *op. cit.*, volume II, p. 91.
9. —, Autumn-Winter *op. cit.*, p. 135.
10. Mackenzie, *op. cit.*, p. 49.
11. —, *ibid.*, p. 54.
12. —, p. 50.
13. —, p. 10.
14. —, p. 2.
15. —, p. 16.
16. Henderson, *op. cit.*, p. 147.
17. *ibid.*, p. 129.
18. Mackenzie, *op. cit.*, p. 15.
19. *ibid.*, p. 15.
20. —, *ibid.*, p. 17. [Issa.]
21. —, *ibid.*
22. —, *ibid.*, p. 18.
23. —, *ibid.*, p. 19
24. —, *ibid.*, p. 21.
25. —, *ibid.*
26. —, *ibid.*, p. 18.
27. —, *ibid.*, p. 26.
28. —, *ibid.*, p. 28.
29. —, *ibid.*, p. 33 [the original quote says "baulked" not "bilked"].
30. Henderson, *op. cit.*, p. 140.
31. —, *ibid.*, p. 150.
32. Mackenzie, *op. cit.*, p. 35.
33. Blyth, *A History of Haiku*, Volume I, p. 422.
34. —, *ibid.*, p. 397.
35. Mackenzie, *op. cit.*, p. 35.
36. Henderson, *op. cit.*, p. 145.
37. Mackenzie, *op. cit.*, p. 36.
38. —, *ibid.*, p. 37.
39. —, *ibid.*, p. 38.
40. —, *ibid.*
41. —, *ibid.*, p. 89.
42. —, *ibid.*, p. 39.
43. Henderson, *op. cit.*, p. 133.
44. Blyth, *Haiku*, Summer-Autumn, *op. cit.*, p. 192.
45. Mackenzie, *op. cit.*, p. 52.
46. Blyth, Autumn-Winter *op. cit.*, p. 78.
47. —, *ibid.*, p. 81.
48. —, *ibid.*, p. 80.
49. Blyth, *A History of Haiku*, Vol. II, *op cit.*, p. 71.
50. Henderson, *op.cit.*, p. 133.
51. Blyth, *Japanese Life and Character in Senryu* (Japan, Hokuseido, 1960), p. 151.
52. —, *op. cit.*, Vol. III, p. 214.
53. Mackenzie, *op. cit.*, p. 5.
54. —, *ibid.*, p. 43.
55. —, p. 44.
56. Blyth, *op. cit.*, *Haiku*, Vol. II, p. 351.
57. Mackenzie, *op. cit.*, p. 46.

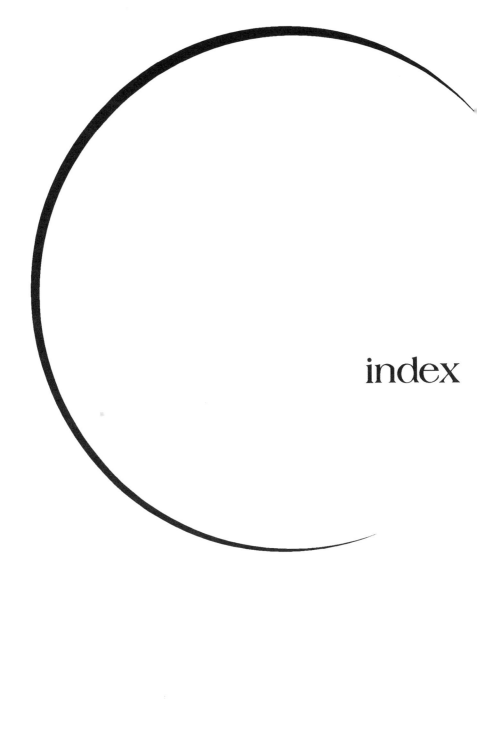

index

index of authors

credits

al li—"accident site" *Modern Haiku XXIX:1;* **Aikens**—"inchworm" *Haiku sans Frontières;* **Alma**—"wind lifting" *Haiku Headlines 107;* **Beary**—"early spring walk" *From a Kind Neighbor;* **Beatty**—"wind against" *Mayfly 24;* **Berry**—"autumn" *Mainichi Daily News;* "impressive name" *Light and Shadow;* "late afternoon" *Penumbra 1998;* **Better**—"last day of the year" *Raw NervZ IV:4;* "only the groundhog" *FrogpondXXI:1;* **Board**—"the year's first" *Absence of Cows;* **Borne**—"after the shooting" *Absence of Cows;* **Bostok**—"test negative" *ant ant ant ant ant 3;* **Brooks**—"funeral procession" *Henderson Haiku Contest 1998;* "behind her" *Raw Nervz V:2;* "estate auction—" *Modern Haiku XXIX:3;* **Buettner**—"In the Hospice" *Modern Haiku XXIX:3;* **Cecilione**—"pausing between chapters" *Frogpond XXI:2;* **Chang**—"starry night—" *Frogpond XXI:1;* **Chessing**—"years in therapy" *Hummingbird 8:3;* **Childs**—"firefly viewing" *The Second New Zealand Haiku Anthology;* **Chula**—"late into the night" *Henderson Haiku Contest 1998;* **Clausen**—"Memorial Day" *Frogpond XXI:3;* "under the manhole" *Frogpond XX:3;* **Cobb**—"drip by drip" *Haiku sans Frontières;* **Compton**—"motor stilled…" *South by Southeast V:1;* **Currier**—"the gift of a book" *Frogpond XX:3;* **Dalton**—"spring cleaning" *Light and Shadow;* **Daniel**—"a bitter rain" *The Iron Book of Haiku;* **Davie**—"on the path" *From a Kind Neighbor;* **Day**—"alone…" *Frogpond XX:3;* "Snapshot" *Frogpond XXI:2;* **Detrick**—"empty house" *Absence of Cows;* **Dillon**—"drought's end:" *Modern Haiku XXIX:2;* **Doty**—"winter night" *Nose to Nose;* **Dullaghan**—"on the teacher's apple" *The Iron Book of Haiku;* **Einbond**—"peeling the apple" *Mainichi Daily News;* **Emrich**—"dusk—" *Cricket;* **Evetts**—"his dust mask" *Absence of Cows;* "clocks turned back" *Frogpond XXI:1;* **Fessler**—"diving catch" *Modern Haiku XXIX:1;* **Fuhringer**—"nightfall" *Brady Senryu Contest 1998;* **Gallagher**—"blowing out" *Brady Senryu Contest 1998;* **Gay**—"Fading light—" *Penumbra 1998;* "Snapshot" *Frogpond XXI:2;* **Gershator**—"at the flea market" *Brady Senryu Contest 1998;* **Gilbert**—"empty chair" *South by Southeast V:3;* **Gilliland**—"abandoned chapel" *Modern Haiku XXIX:1;* **Glover**—"On the great penis" *The Iron Book of Haiku;* **Gonzales**—"Into Sunlight" *Azami 47;* **Gorman**—"last hike" *South by Southeast V:1;* **Gurga**—"a sunken barge" *Modern Haiku XXIX:3;* "the smell of the iron" "winter prairie—" *Fresh Scent;* **Hardenbrook**—"classroom mineral chart" *Frogpond XXI:2;* "what is whose…" *Frogpond XXI:1;* "at the window" *Raw Nervz IV:4;* "autumn leaves" *Modern Haiku XXIX:1;* "poetry reading" *Raw Nervz IV:4;* "construction job" *Modern Haiku XXIX:2;* **Heitmeyer**—"cheap paperback" *Modern Haiku XXIX:2;* **Herold**—"curling paint" *Modern Haiku XXIX:1;* "driftwood" *South by Southeast V:1;* **Hotham**—"in what's left" *South by Southeast V:2;* "fog" *Haiku sans Frontières;* **houck, jr.**—"at her bedside" *Modern Haiku XXIX:1;* "autumn wind" *Modern Haiku XXIX:1;* **Hryciuk**—"hairpin turn" *Spin 31;* **Jackson**—"everywhere" *The Iron Book of Haiku;* **Kacian**—"rocking" *Hummingbird 9:1;* "morning dew" *Six Directions;* "ground fog" *Six Directions;* "cold snap—" *Mayfly 24;* "Custom" *Modern Haiku XXIX:3;* "The Curve of the Air" *Six Directions;* **Kanda**—"facing the wall" "entering my" *An Owl Hoots;* **Keener**—"an old schoolyard" *Shiki Internet Haiku Salon;* **Ketchek**—"my father" *Frogpond XX:3;* "so much" *Persimmon 1:2;* **Kimmel**—"after a hard look" *Frogpond XXI:2;* **Krivcher**—"Writing from the Monkey Face" *Frogpond XX:3;* **Leibman**—"even after Christmas" *Frogpond XXI:1;* **Lucas**—"morning mist" *The Iron Book of Haiku;* **Lyles**—"I brush" *Frogpond XXI:2;* "North Star obscured" *Modern Haiku XXIX:1;* **m.**—"falling leaves" *Modern Haiku XXIX:1;* **Mair**—"Day Out" *WinterSpin 28;* **Makiko**—"home from abroad" *Modern Haiku XXIX:1;* **McLaughlin**—"aunt's diamond ring" *Modern Haiku XXIX:1;* **McLeod**—"the updraft" *Acorn 1;* "long wait over—" *Shiki Internet Haiku Salon;* **Mena**—"as the Market tumbles" *Cricket;* **Missias**—"new grave" *Modern Haiku XXIX:1;* **Moreau**—"waking in the meadow" *Hummingbird 8:3;* **Nelson**—"Verdun" *Modern Haiku XXIX:1;* **Ness**—"Christmas Eve—" *Modern Haiku XXIX:2;* "after all these years" *Frogpond XXI:2;* **Neubauer**— "The Goldfish Vendor" *Journey to the Interior;* **Nilic**—"moonlight" *Frogpond XXI:2;* **Noyes**—"evening light" *Modern Haiku XXIX:1;* "waterfall" *WinterSpin 1998;* "Poppies, Simplicity, Spirit & Spiess" *Hobo Spring 1998;* "Great Haiku with Sabi" *Frogpond XXI:1;* **Okolski**—"DOA" *Frogpond XXI:1;* **Osterhaus**—"abandoned farm—" *Hacket Haiku Contest 1998;* **Painting**—"ending" *South by Southeast V:3;* **Parry**—"suddenly I realize" *Frogpond XX:3;* **Patrick**—"fireflies" *Brady Senryu Contest 1998;* "after ringing it up" *Absence of Cows;* **Peel**—"wintry evening" *The Iron Book of Haiku;* **Pettit**—"the charity collector" *The Iron Book of Haiku;* **Porad**—"double plot" *Modern Haiku XXIX:3;* **Prime**—"Day Out" *Winter Spin 1998;* **Pupello**—"simmering stew" *The Saxman's Case;* "this heat" *The Saxman's Case;* "wedding vows" *The Saxman's Case;* "Wall Street gym" *Modern Haiku XXIX:2;* **Purington**—"bundles in woods" *Hummingbird 8:3;* **Rabkin**—"after coming in" *Heron Quarterly 2:2;* **Ramsey**—"pulling gate nails" *Hummingbird 9:1;***Realey**—"still in my suit" *Frogpond XXI:2;* **Romano**—"Sunday morning" *black bough 12;* **Ross**—"coming to rest" *Frogpond XX:2;* **Rotella**—"On our short walk" *Modern Haiku XXIX:3;* **Russell**—"eggs sunny-side up…" *Raw Nervz V:2;* **Ryan**—"gentle rain" *Modern Haiku XXIX:1;* **Saunders**—"the funeral director" *Haiku Canada 9:3;* **Scanzello**—"hiking hand in hand" *Frogpond XXI:1;* **Schofield**—"children in the band" *Blithe Spirit 8:2;* **Shafii**—"convalescence" *Modern Haiku XXIX:1;* **Sheirer**—"talking in her sleep" *Made from Icicles;* **Sherman**—"winter light" *Modern Haiku XXIX:2;* "long meeting" *Shiki Internet Haiku Salon;* **Sohne**—"scenic hillside" *Absence of Cows;* **Spriggs**—"my head" *Sparrow 1997-98;* **St Jacques**—"first snow" *Haiku sans Frontières;* **Steele**—"shipping oars" *The Iron Book of Haiku;* **Stefanac**—"frost predicted" *Mayfly 24;* **Stevenson**—"between my rush to be ready" *Modern Haiku XXIX:1;* "at the urinal" *Frogpond XXI:1;* "the mirror" *Frogpond XXI:2;* "The Bow Unravels" *Raw Nervz IV:4;* **Stuart-Powles**—"father's funeral" *Frogpond XX:3;* **Summers**—"Into Sunlight" *Azami 47;* **Swede**—"Medieval town:" *Still 2:4;* **Swist**—"dry season" *Raw Nervz V:2;* **Tasker**—"in the park" *The Iron Book of Haiku;* **Tico**—"Christmas Eve…" "Memorial Day" "The next morning" *SPRING MORNING SUN;* "Personification" *Frogpond XXI:1;* **Tomczak**—"family reunion" *Brady Senryu Contest 1998;* **Trammell**—"Haiku: Toward an

Organic Definition for the West" *Modern Haiku XXIX: 3*; **Trumbull**—"grocery line" *Frogpond XX: 3*; **van den Heuvel**—"after the grand slam" *Absence of Cows*; **Vayman**—"autumn evening" *Henderson Haiku Contest 1998*; **Virgil**—"Issa: The Uses of Adversity" *South by Southeast V: 1-3*; **Volz**—"able to move" *Frogpond XXI: 2*; **Walsh**—"talking to myself" *To Find a Rainbow*; **Ward, D.**—"new employee" *Raw NervZ IV: 4*; **Ward, L.**—"on the way" *Frogpond XXI: 1*; **Watsky**—"science museum" *Frogpond XX: 3*; **Welch**—"sudden lightning"—*Modern Haiku XXIX: 2*; "gridlock" *Modern Haiku XXIX: 1*; "hospital room" *South by Southeast V: 1*; **White**—"Drawing Down the Moon" *Frogpond XXI: 2*; **Wicker**—"waitress serving crabs" *Frogpond XXI: 1*; **Witkin**—"through tree shadows" *Frogpond XXI: 1*; "her Christmas bonus" *Raw Nervz V: 1*; "The Bow Unravels" *Raw Nervz IV: 4*; **Wright**—"Just enough of rain" "The Christmas season:" "The crow flew so fast" *Haiku: This Other World*; **Youmans**—"Hale-Bopp" *Modern Haiku XXIX: 2*; "Sunday Visits" *Journey to the Interior*; **Young**—"walking together" *Frogpond XXI: 1*; **Zackowitz**—"midnight" *Cricket*.

Books:

Absence of Cows, ed. Spring Street Haiku Group (Spring Street Members' Anthology, New York, 1998). $5

An Owl Hoots, Sosuke Kanda (Heirakuji-shoten, Japan, 1998). ISBN 4-8313-0723-8. ¥2500

Fresh Scent, Lee Gurga (Brooks Books, Decatur IL, 1998). ISBN 0-913719-86-2. $20

From a Kind Neighbor, ed. John Stevenson (Haiku Society of America Members' Anthology, Haiku Society of America, Nassau NY, 1997). ISBN 0-9631467-5-0. $9

Haiku sans frontières: une anthologie mondiale, ed. André Duhaime. ISBN 2-922109-14-3. $30 Canadian

Haiku: This Other World, Richard Wright (Arcade Publishing, New York, 1998). ISBN 1-55970-445-4. $20

Journey to the Interior: North American Versions of Haibun, ed. Bruce Ross (Charles Tuttle Publishers, Boston MA, 1998). ISBN 0-8048-3159-9. $21.95

Light and Shadow, ed. Garry Gay (Haiku Society of America Members's Anthology, Haiku Society of America in conjunction with Press Here, Foster City CA, 1998). ISBN 0-9631467-6-9. $7

Made from Icicles, John Sheirer (First Blade Publishers, Belpre OH, 1998). $8

Nose to Nose, Gene Doty (Brooks Books, Decatur IL, 1998). ISBN 0-913719-97-9. $8

Six Directions, Jim Kacian (La Alameda Press, Albuquerqu NM, 1998). ISBN 0-9631909-4-6. $10

SPRING MORNING SUN, Tom Tico (Morris Publishing, Kearney NE, 1998). ISBN 1-57502-711-9. $12

The Iron Book of Haiku, ed. David Cobb & Martin Lucas (Iron Press, Northumberland, Great Britain, 1998). ISBN 0-906228-67-0. £6.50

The Saxman's Case, Anthony J. Pupello (Red Moon Press, Winchester VA, 1998). ISBN 0-9657818-6-0. $10

The Second New Zealand Haiku Anthology, ed. Cyril Childs (The New Zealand Poetry Society, Inc., Wellington NZ, 1998). ISBN 0-473-05374-8. $10

To Find a Rainbow, Phyllis Walsh (Hummingbird Press, Richland Center WI, 1998). $10

Periodicals:

Acorn (ed. A. C. Missias, 436 Spruce St. #2, Philadelphia PA 19106 USA)

ant ant ant ant ant (ed. chris gordon, PO Box 16177, Oakland CA 94610 USA)

Azami (ed. Ikkoku Santo, c/o Santcel, CPO Box 361, Osaka 530-91 Japan)

black bough (ed. Charles Easter, 188 Grove Street #1, Somerville NJ 08876 USA)

Blithe Spirit (ed. Caroline Gourlay, Hill House Farm, Knighton, Powys LD7 1NA Great Britain)

Frogpond (ed. Jim Kacian, PO Box 2461, Winchester VA 22604-1661 USA)

Haiku Canada Newsletter (ed. LeRoy Gorman, 51 Graham West, Napanee, Ontario K7R 2J6 Canada)

Haiku Headlines (ed. David Priebe, 1347 W. 71st Street, Los Angeles CA 90044 USA)

Heron Quarterly (ed. Carolyn Thomas, PO Box 1175, Borrego Springs CA 92004 USA)

Hobo (ed. Janice Bostok, Campbell's Road, Dungay NSW 2484 Australia)

Hummingbird (ed. Phyllis Walsh, PO Box 96, Richland Center WI 53581 USA)

Mainichi Daily News (ed. Kazuo Sato, 1-1-1 Hitotsubashi, 1-chome, Chiyoda-ku, Tokyo 100-51 Japan)

Mayfly (ed. Randy Brooks, 4634 Hale Drive, Decatur IL 62526 USA)

Modern Haiku (ed. Robert Spiess, PO Box 1752, Madison WI 53701 USA)

Penumbra (ed. John Flood, PO Box 940, Manotick, Ontario K4M 1A8 Canada)

Persimmon (ed. Mary C. Taylor, 19626 Damman, Harper Woods MI 48225 USA)

Raw NervZ (ed. Dorothy Howard, 67 Court Street, Aylmer (QC) J9H 4M1 Canada)

South by Southeast (ed. Jim Kacian, PO Box 2461, Winchester VA 22604-1661 USA)

Sparrow (ed. Marijan Cekolj, Smerovisce 24, 10430 Samobor Croatia)

Spin (ed. various, 7 Megan Avenue, Pakuranga, Auckland New Zealand)

Still (ed. ai li, 49 England's Lane, London NW3 4YD England)

Contests:

The Gerald Brady Senryu Contest (Haiku Society of America)

The Harold G. Henderson Haiku Contest (Haiku Society of America)

The James W. Hackett Haiku Competition (British Haiku Society)

On-Line Sources:

Cricket

Shiki Internet Haiku Salon